KEEP IN STEP

Keep
in
Step

JOHN & SUE RITTER

KINGSWAY PUBLICATIONS
EASTBOURNE

ISBN 0 86065 464 8

Unless otherwise indicated, biblical quotations are from
the Holy Bible: New International Version, copyright ©
International Bible Society 1973, 1978, 1984.

Front cover design by Vic Mitchell

Printed in Great Britain for
KINGSWAY PUBLICATIONS LTD
Lottbridge Drove, Eastbourne, E. Sussex BN23 6NT by
Richard Clay Ltd, Bungay, Suffolk.
Typeset by Nuprint Ltd, Harpenden, Herts.

To all the people whose houses we have stayed in over the years, and who have kept us up until the early hours of the morning discussing issues like these!

In particular: Ian and Maggie Clyne, Rev Tony and Chris Ashton, Keith and Margaret Lodge, David and Liz Smith, Steve and Lyn Porter, and Phil and Shirley Rees.

Contents

Introduction

Hey! What's all this? She's written all these books by herself and suddenly she needs a helping hand? Could this be a publicity stunt?

No way. John and I have changed our ministry just lately to encompass youth weekends and youth conferences involving a good deal of seminars. This has brought about many requests for notes of what we have said, and copies of certain quotes, idiotic sketches and quizzes. Now, John delivers more than half of these seminars, but to put it in his words: 'If I wrote it, it would be like reading a formal letter from your bank manager!' We didn't think you'd relish that too much, so we put our heads together and came up with this great idea of my translating what he says into the usual bright cheerful laugh-a-minute style you are used to!

We hope the finished product will be incredibly useful to you, whether you are a youth leader or a teenager.

Sue Ritter

I

Practical Witnessing

The approach

People who know me will tell you that one-to-one witnessing is *not* my speciality. Everyone has things they're good at, but when it comes to this I have to try very hard. And I try to work out all sorts of devious ways to make it easy on myself! This chapter is aimed at people like me. So all you other folk out there who find this kind of thing easy can lend an ear of sympathy to the rest of us!

For me, one of the worst things in the world is to approach a total stranger, for whatever reason. I'm sure you have had times when you are in a strange town and if you are *ever* going to find Barclays Bank before 3.30 pm, then you are going to have to ask someone. So how come you always ask someone who says, 'Sorry, I don't live here either!' That remark leaves you feeling a total idiot and twice as anxious about asking someone else. Have you ever watched *Sorry!* on the telly? It's about a little bloke who almost apologizes for living. I can just imagine him walking up to someone and saying, 'Sorry, excuse me. I know you're probably in too much of a

hurry to help me, sorry, but I don't suppose you know
...no, why shouldn't you? You probably don't live
here. Sorry about that. No, it's quite all right. I'll ask
someone else. Sorry to have bothered you, silly of
me....'

Now think! If we can get into that kind of state about
finding the local bank, how on earth are we going to
approach people and tell them about Jesus? Sometimes
I think that whoever invented open air and door-to-
door work wants his head examined! But there you are,
it is part and parcel of the Christian scene and sometime
or other we are going to get pulled into it. So how are
we going to survive?

The escape route

One of the best ways of conducting an hour or so of
personal witnessing on the streets is by means of a
survey. Now, you must have had people coming up to
you in the street, or to your front door, telling you that
they are from such and such a company and they would
like your opinion on a certain product. Yes? I thought
so. Anyway, we had a lady knocking on our door the
other day, and she wanted my opinion on tea. Yes,
that's right, tea. She was doing a national survey on
what brand of tea we drink and why we drink it, etc.

To start with, she asked me if I could recognize a
brand of tea if she described the advert to me. Fun, eh?
So there we were laughing about the chimps in one
advert and the people who go 'oooh' in another. It was
just like being on a quiz show! From there, she showed
me some pictures on packets of tea with the brand
name cut out. Could I name them now? We went on to
the advantages of tea-bags over tea leaves, and a
pleasant time was had by all. Yet all I was doing was
talking about *tea*! How uninspiring, how tedious, but

it was made to look attractive and fun to talk about. Am I getting through?

People are often willing to give you all the time in the world to answer questions on a survey. They are happy to give their own super-interesting opinion on just about any subject you care to name, and that includes Christianity! What a great way to approach someone you don't know: 'Excuse me, Sir. I wonder if you would like to give some opinions for our survey?' It's like a magnet!

So now we need to devise a way of making a survey interesting. What shall we ask them? Let's start with one they all have an answer for: 'When did you last go to church?' That should set them thinking. Now, rather than writing down their answer, it's more professional to have little boxes by the side of the question for you to tick. For example: A. Every week. B. Once a month. C. Weddings or funerals. D. Other. (It's always worth having an 'other' box because there's usually one smart alec who will have an answer you haven't covered.) Having answered this one question, you may find Joe Public giving you more details about his experience of church, in which case you might not even need to go any further with the survey! But let's press on, we need questions that make Joe feel that his opinion really counts and as far as the Christian public go, it does, very much.

Let's get a rough survey together then. Now I realize that some of these questions might not be suitable for your particular area, or you may be able to find some more relevant ones. The idea behind a survey/opinion poll is to let the people have a chance to say what *they* think, and then at anytime during the proceedings you may find a chance to join in and put your point of view across.

Tick relevant box

1. Do you ever go to church?
   - A. Every week ☐
   - B. Sometimes ☐
   - C. Weddings, etc ☐
   - D. Other ☐

2. What was your impression of the service?
   - A. Very good ☐
   - B. All right ☐
   - C. Boring ☐
   - D. Other ☐

3. What do you think could have helped you enjoy church more?

   . . . .
   . . . .
   . . . .

4. What role do you think the church should play today?
   - A. Religious ☐
   - B. Social ☐
   - C. Moral ☐
   - D. Other ☐

5. Would you consider yourself to be a Christian?
   - A. Yes ☐
   - B. No ☐
   - C. We all are ☐
   - D. Other ☐

6. What is your impression of Jesus?
   - A. Personal ☐
   - B. Remote ☐
   - C. Human ☐
   - D. Other ☐

7. If you could get to know God personally, would you be interested?
   - A. Yes ☐
   - B. No ☐
   - C. If it would help me ☐
   - D. Other ☐

Don't forget that you have told people that this is a survey, and you will therefore be expected to discuss your findings in some way or other. Maybe you could print them in your church magazine and send the results to your local paper, or even give the magazine out during the following weeks, explaining to the folk in town that it's the results of last week's survey.

I'm making this up as I go along, but I quite like the idea of publishing the results in your local rag. As I said earlier, there might well be things going on in your town that you could relate to in the survey, and this all helps to create local interest. Oh yes, and don't forget your local radio station either. Why not go round town with a tape recorder, recording people's opinions, and put together a decent Christian programme for your local radio station?

It's a fact that people love to tell you what they think, and this kind of approach can be used on doorsteps or right in the middle of town. I'm sure that before you know it you will find yourself entering into all sorts of discussions.

The wrong impression

OK, now we have looked at one way of approaching people, let's laugh at ourselves and look at the wrong way of doing things. A lot can be learnt about the right way by looking at the wrong way. We'll start by giving you a sketch that can be used in your church or youth group. It gives ample room for discussion afterwards.

The Ronnie and Eric sketch

Very few props are needed for this sketch. In fact, you can get away with two chairs and a table. The scene is a local pub where Eric is sitting having a quiet drink.

He's an amiable sort of chap, easy to get on with and
rather docile. Ronnie, on the other hand, is a bit erratic
and he's just become a Christian. He's dying to tell Eric
all about it, but isn't quite sure how to approach the
subject.

(*Eric seated at table. Enter Ronnie.*)

ERIC: Ronnie!

RONNIE: Eric!

ERIC: How you been keeping then? How's things then?

RONNIE: Lovely, Eric. Couldn't be better. In fact I've...
er....

ERIC: What? Won the pools have you, Ron?

RONNIE: (*Getting irritated.*) No, no! Er...I've become...
er...become a er....

ERIC: (*Surprised.*) What Ron? A married man, eh?!
(*Nudges him.*)

RONNIE: No...no....I've become a er....

ERIC: (*Puzzled.*) What? You've become a....Here,
you're not a....

RONNIE: (*Hastily.*) No! No! I've become a (*mumbles*)
Christian, Eric.

ERIC: Pardon? I can't hear you.

RONNIE: I said, I've become a (*mumbles again*)
Christian, Eric.

ERIC: Get off! You—a Christian? Well, well, who'd have
guessed it? (*Smiles at him.*) So, what's that all about
then, Ron?

RONNIE: Well you...er...that is I not you...er...well I
go er...

ERIC: Red? You've gone a bit red at the moment, Ron.

RONNIE: (*Getting more confused.*) No, I go to...
er...

ERIC: (*Guessing patiently.*) Evening classes? What?

RONNIE: No, I go to...er...

ERIC: Bed early on Sundays?

RONNIE: No! I go to church...er...it's part of...er...

ERIC: *(Brightening.)* Part of the new social club down the road, is it?

RONNIE: No, it's part of being a Christian, going to church is.

ERIC: *(Interested.)* Get off! What a sort of club, is it?

RONNIE: Well, not really, but I suppose it could be seen that way. We do a lot of...er...

ERIC: People out of their money, Ron?

RONNIE: No, we do a lot of...er...

ERIC: *(Getting frustrated.)* Skateboarding? Model-making? Fish frying? What? What?

RONNIE: No, we do a lot of singing. Y'know, choruses....

ERIC: *(Puzzled.)* Why? Don't they know no verses then?

RONNIE: *(Thinking it was a joke.)* Very good, Eric. No really, we sing lots of lively songs about...er...

ERIC: Six times till you know all the words, eh?

RONNIE: No! We sing about loving your neighbour and y'know....

ERIC: *(Gives him a nudge.)* Wouldn't mind loving my neighbour, Ronnie.

RONNIE: No?

ERIC: No, Ron. She's blonde, about twenty-one....

RONNIE: Now, Eric, you're not taking me seriously! *(Looks solemn.)* You know, being a Christian is great, it's not all *Stars on Sunday*, you know.

ERIC: Innit?

RONNIE: No, there's a lot of er...a lot of...er....

ERIC: It about, eh?

RONNIE: *(Doubly seriously.)* No. I was going to say that there's a lot of...joy in being a Christian, Eric.

ERIC: *(Puzzled.)* In what way then?

RONNIE: Well, we don't all wear black you know...er... nothing like that. In fact we...er...we wear er....

ERIC: *(Frowning.)* Red? Blue? Orange? What?

RONNIE: No, no! We wear what we like. It's not a set of rigid rules and regulations. Oh no, in fact it's very free....

ERIC: And that's what makes everything joyful is it then? Having everything free?

RONNIE: No, I mean free as in not stiff and starchy! You'd probably enjoy it yourself, you'll have to... er....

ERIC: Not wear black, eh? *(Laughs jovially.)*

RONNIE: No, you'll have to come one Sunday. It'll er... er....

ERIC: Make a change from the pub!

RONNIE: *(Grasping at any straw.)* Yes!

ERIC: So that's it then. Christianity is going to church and enjoying yourself?

RONNIE: That's right, Eric. *(Stands up and makes his way to the door.)* Anyway, I'd best be off. See you around. Bye.

ERIC: *(Smiling.)* Yeh, see you, Ronnie! Going off to church for a sing-song, eh?

RONNIE: *(From the door.)* Er... er... yeh.
(Pause.)

ERIC: *(Turning his chair to face audience.)* S'funny—I always thought it had something to do with Jesus.

Yes, I know, you have seen similar sketches on *The Two Ronnies* and *Alas Smith and Jones*. I think that the reason why these kinds of comedies are so successful, is because we all love to listen in on other people's conversation. There is something that draws you to a conversation, and it has an impact that one person addressing you doesn't have. Again, this sketch is just an example and I'm sure you can do tons better. All I'm trying to do is give you the ideas and the reasoning behind them.

Look at soap operas. Once again you have that 'fly on the wall' situation, looking in on other people's lives and work places, and either identifying with them, or wishing you were like them. You can't tell me you haven't wanted to live in the style of the Dynasty cast just for one day... if only to see what caviar tastes like!

Assuming now that you have performed this little sketch to a Christian audience, you could either leave it at that, or take it further. The sketch leaves itself open to discussion which can be done in several ways. You could split into groups and give each group some questions about Ronnie and Eric. For example: Where did Ronnie first start to go wrong? Should he have spoken about something else first? *Or*, if your actors are willing, you could use them as a sort of 'action replay', getting them to act out certain parts of the conversation and then freeze at the end. You then ask the whole group what they thought about that part, as though they were watching a video clip.

It will be easy to identify with Ronnie in one way or another. We might not be like him in character, but we have all had the experience of wanting to witness to someone and trying to find the perfect moment. Most people will agree that the longer you talk about Christianity without talking about Jesus, the harder it becomes to talk about him at all.

The right impression

First impressions are important in just about every area of life. What you've got to say for yourself and how much you know is irrelevant if people are put off by what they see. What do they think when they see you? What do they think when they hear you? Well, not many of us really get a chance to find out the answers to these questions as they are normally the kind of things that are talked about *after* we have gone! On the other hand I don't suppose many folk would really enjoy hearing what other people think of them. If you sat down and wrote a little composition about yourself, about character, etc., and then asked a friend to do the same about you, I wonder how the notes would compare? Maybe your friend would see your 'piercing blue eyes' as 'sly and shifty' and your 'forthright manner' as 'rude'! Just think, that 'friendly manner' could be interpreted as 'nosey'. Awful, isn't it? It's not that I think we should all be going round picking holes in each other, but maybe it's time that we saw ourselves as the people on the street see us—especially if we want to witness to them.

This is your life

I said earlier that we all enjoy hearing what other people think, and here is a unique opportunity for you to find out what they think of John and me! (Yes, I thought that would make you sit a bit straighter... gossip coming up!) It happened like this....

We were at a school in Peterborough a while back and we had been booked to stay there for the whole week. We played in assemblies and talked to the pupils in lessons; we played to them at lunchtime and during their music lessons. All in all, they got to know us quite well (I could even remember some of their names by Friday!). Anyway, towards the end of the week, we were sitting in the staffroom trying to avoid the coffee (why is it always that chicory stuff?) when a teacher came in carrying a pile of essays. She sat down beside us and dumped the essays on our laps. 'Here you are,' she said. 'Our third years have been writing essays on their impressions of you over the week.'

You know, to look down at a pile of criticisms and

witty remarks and know that they are all about you, is a weird sensation. Half of you is yelling out, 'Read them now! Immediately!' while the other half is shrieking, 'No! Wait until you're outside the building where no one can see your reaction!'

In the end we read them in the staffroom, and as you can imagine, it made very interesting reading. It also made us realize that people look in different places for Christianity.

Look at these two comments from the third years:

'We were expecting a few old fogies wailing hymns.... We definitely got a shock!'

'Before the actual performance, there was talk of it being another rubbish band that the teachers had dragged in to make assembly even more boring than usual.... But what a surprise!'

I think the response of these two people was favourable, but what a shame that their ideas of a 'Christian band' were so bad. Looking at the content of these responses, it's obvious that they equated Christian music with 'boring', 'rubbish' and 'old'. Mainly I suppose because the only thing they have to equate it with apart from *The Rock Gospel Show* (which has certainly made life easier for us) is *Songs of Praise*, or situation comedies involving doddery old vicars, or any other TV programme with a Christian link.

To some of those kids we were a shock, to others a surprise. Either way we held their attention and that's good.

Anyway, these comments made us realize that if you are going to stand up for Jesus, then you are going to be looked at and criticized from every angle.

Years ago I used to write for a magazine called *Buzz* and the object of my column was to make people sit up a bit. I began to get a reputation for being outspoken and letters started coming in to the mag both complaining and cheering me on. I wrote one particular column about TV and said how much I enjoyed watching American 'trash', for example *Starsky and Hutch* (today of course it would be *Miami Vice*). I really went to town on that article—laughing at people who bought large expensive colour TVs just to 'watch the news' when a paper would have been much cheaper! Love it or hate it—people took notice and reacted!

You see, the point I'm trying to make is that unless you are loud and overstate your case, no one will listen. Now I'm not suggesting for a minute that you rush out and join a Christian rock band, or start writing outspoken columns in magazines, but I *am* suggesting that you make your point.

John and I witness in a loud, colourful way, but you can be just as effective in a different way. Look at this comment from a pupil:

'It felt weird that a "good group" playing rock music had a religious meaning.'

The main point here is that they thought we were good and that surprised them. Now, I wonder what you are good at? These reactions could be accredited to you:

'He's a Christian? How can he be? He's the best accountant we've got!'

'I often wondered how she kept her cool while playing such good tennis—and now she tells me it's due to her being a Christian!'

Isn't it annoying that people think of Christians as seconds? Have a look at yourself, find out what you're good at and give the glory to God. Astound your friends!

OK, back to the essays. Here's a thought-provoking one:

'I think a group like this should not spend so much time and money on expensive equipment, clothes and haircuts.'

To give this pupil credit, I think I should point out that this was written in pre-Band Aid days! But there you have it; to the outsider a Christian is someone who should be void of all possessions and should not care about their looks. It makes you realize that there are a lot of barriers to break down before you can get through to people, doesn't it? For us, the money question comes up time and time again, mainly because we are on the school stage with thousands of pounds' worth of equipment. One of the first questions we are asked is how much the equipment is worth and how we manage to afford it! Happily we get a good chance to explain the answer to them. Basically, to do a good job, you have to have the best tools. If we swapped our synthesizers and guitars for imitations, the sound we produced would be cheap and nasty, and the credibility of what we are doing for the Lord would go down the drain.

Of course, if we got rid of the music altogether, then we would be ridding ourselves of the very thing that attracts young people to us. If we just turned up in assembly and preached, I'm sure you would almost be able to hear their brains clicking off. When we ask them what they would prefer, 100% of them prefer us to include music!

So, as you can see, non-Christians are full of pre-conceived ideas when it comes to what a Christian is all about.

Back to practicalities

Right! Enough of the 'how to'. Let's finish with a bit of practical work. When you are next together with your youth group, perhaps you could try something out. First of all, have a good chat about witnessing and the kind of thing I've written about in this chapter, then get yourself into groups of three or four.

This idea may sound simplistic but having tried it on numerous youth groups, it has proved to be amazingly successful. What I want you to do is this:

One of you has to volunteer to be a non-Christian. (If you have a non-Christian in your little group so much the better, but if not you need a volunteer.) Now, the other two or three have got to try and convince you that the Christian life is the only life worth living! Meanwhile you'll be putting up as many obstacles as you can. (Perhaps I should warn you at this stage, that when the whole thing gets going fisti-cuffs are against the rules!)

There are several really good things that come out of this exercise:

1. The person playing the non-Christian will be able to remember what it feels like to be outside God's kingdom.

2. If the person in the role of non-Christian actually *is*, then you will find them very happy to defend their title!

3. The Christians will come up against a lot of questions they feel inadequate to answer.

4. It gets the evangelistic blood flowing!

After fifteen minutes or so, call the room to order and discuss the questions you couldn't answer. This is where youth leaders need to be very clever and knowledgeable! Believe me, the aftermath of the group sessions can go on all night as people come up against, 'Why is there so much suffering?', 'Where is heaven anyway?', 'How do you know the Bible is real?' and 'Why doesn't God show himself?'

We have found that this kind of session gives Christians a chance to ask questions that have been bothering them, but have maybe been too embarrassed to ask about for themselves.

Then, having gone through all the awkward questions, it should nearly be time to get out into your world and try it out on other people. Jesus said, 'Go into all the world,' and he meant *your* world: where your friends are, your workmates, your relations, your neighbourhood.

Go get 'em!

2

Your Responsibility

Hang on a minute! I know you don't like the title of this chapter, but that's exactly why it's here! There's not a lot of point in reading all the other chapters if you're not interested in what God has to say about your responsibility to the people outside of his kingdom, right?

The first chapter in the book was called 'Practical Witnessing' which is all well and fine if you feel so burdened for the world that you must go out and preach the gospel. But most of us need the challenge first, and that's what this chapter is all about.

The survey

Get ready to cringe. This survey was taken quite recently, and it's one that tries to convey the situation of Christianity in Britain.

Did you know that in a recent survey of church members...

1. 10% cannot be found anywhere.
2. 20% never attend a church service.

3. 25% admit they never pray.
4. 35% never read their Bibles.
5. 40% never contribute to the church.
6. 60% never study religious material.
7. 75% never assume responsibility in their church.
8. 85% never invited anyone to their church.
9. 95% never won another person to Christ.
10. 100% expected to go to heaven.

I wonder where you started to loosen your tie or fidget with your fingernails when you read this? Yes, it's about us!

The notes for this particular subject have been written by John and then rewritten by me, so it contains quite a lot of how John himself felt called by God to evangelize. It's an important chapter and I pray that the Lord will speak to you through it.

Our responsibility

Isn't it strange how we all want the privileges of being a Christian and yet we shun our responsibilities? We want all the fun and everything, but without the effort. And, of course, while we are sitting around smiling and singing 'I am H.A.P.P.Y.' people who don't know Jesus are losing their souls. Take another look at that survey. I think the saddest thing about it is that 95% of Christians have never won another person for Christ.

Why on earth is that? How come we openly disobey one of the Lord's commands? He told us to go and preach to all the world and yet we don't do a thing about it. Perhaps we forget that God didn't choose to have angels flying out of heaven to zap people with laser beams and stuff—he chose you and me to go out there and win them with our testimony. When the Lord first spoke to us about it, this is what he said:

Everyone who calls on the name of the Lord will be saved. How, then, can they call on the one they have not believed in? And how can they believe in the one of whom they have not heard? And how can they hear without someone preaching to them? And how can they preach unless they are sent? As it is written, 'How beautiful are the feet of those who bring good news!' (Rom 10:13–15).

It says very directly that the responsibility is ours. The ball is in our court.

The trouble is, we don't feel up to it—we haven't got the confidence in ourselves, or even in God, to believe that we have what it takes. But maybe that's not so bad, because if we can convince ourselves that we're useless then doesn't that let us off the hook? Someone else will have to do it; someone with charisma and style. You know, the outgoing bloke with that 'everybody's pal' look about him.

Your potential

Yes, yours! We would like to show you, in this chapter, that you have all the potential God ever needed and that ordinary people with ordinary lives are just what God is looking for. We want to help to equip you so that when the opportunity comes along for you to be a witness for the Lord, you'll be ready for it. We would hate it if you were to be among that 95% who have never won another person for Jesus. Leading someone into the kingdom of God is the most satisfying and exciting thing that can ever happen to you.

John always says that the first time he led someone to Christ, he was more excited than they were! He was at a Billy Graham Crusade (not *this* time... before that!) and had been trained as a counsellor by the Navigators. They had done a great job on him, but it wasn't until he was confronted with a young lad who wanted to become a Christian, that he had to put his learning into practice. By then, as we've said, John was so excited he felt like it was him who had just become a Christian!

Fear

It is hard to imagine that well-known evangelists and Christian artists could ever be scared when they preach the gospel. But it's silly to think that. Of course they are scared! To tell someone about Jesus carries with it a responsibility, meaning we have to be careful how we handle the situation that God has entrusted to us. So whether the Lord uses you on a one-to-one basis or whether he uses you to preach to the masses, you still have the same choice. You either obey or you don't.

You are scared, I am scared, Luis Palau is scared...but that's no sin! It is no sin to be frightened of what God asks you to do. The Bible is full of scared people who did things for God. The sin is *not doing* what God asks you to. I mean look at poor old Joshua. Moses had just died and God expected Joshua to just step in and take over! We're not talking about a caretaker's job here—we're talking about leading the children of Israel into the promised land! After all the amazing things that Moses had done, Joshua must have been scared stiff! But God said, 'Look, Joshua, I'm here. I'm with you!' And Joshua just picked himself up and got on with the job.

Availability

Joshua made himself available to God, and that's all God asks of any of us. I've said it before and I'll say it again: the only ability God asks of us is availability. Let me tell you about John.

When he was in his teens he was praying one night,

and it was one of those nights when you can't think of anything constructive to pray about. (Oh you have them too, do you?) So, he started reading his Bible and asking the Lord to give him something specific.

Not realizing that this was shaky ground he was treading on, John prayed, 'Lord what do you want me to pray for?' The verse immediately sprang to mind, 'Ask the Lord of the harvest, therefore, to send out workers into his harvest field' (Mt 9:38). So there was John praying his heart out: 'Lord! Send out labourers! The harvest is ripe and the workers so few. Lord, get them out there, we need more labourers.' And then it seemed an even louder voice rang through his mind saying, 'What about *you*, John? Will you go for me?'

And this is where we all react in the same way. 'Who me, Lord? You want me to go out there? I have no talent! I can't preach, I can't sing. I'm shy! There must be a billion more people in the line before me!' John was no different, he tried all these excuses and at the end of them all he came to the same conclusion: 'Well, Lord, maybe I can't do all these things—but I am available. If you think you can use me to go into the world and preach the gospel then I'm here, but that's about it.' But it was enough! As we have already said, availability is all the Lord needs to be able to use you in fantastic ways.

Time and time again

Once John had made his step, the Lord confirmed his word in loads of different ways. It's great that Jesus does that. Over the following weeks there were Bible readings backing up his feelings. There were words of prophecy as the Lord used the gifts of the Spirit to reassure John he had heard right.

People were even coming up to him saying that they

felt he should go to Bible college! All sorts of ways were used to show him that he had heard the Lord right. That's the difference, you see, between someone coming up to you and saying that the Lord has said this, that and the other when Jesus hasn't said anything to you first—rather than this way round which was simply God confirming what he had already told John in the first place. It is just incredible what God can do through you, an ordinary person, if you will only respond to what he is saying. And he's saying, 'Will you trust me? Will you make yourself available for me to use? Will you let me take hold of your life?' If you are willing, tell the Lord right now. Don't miss such an opportunity! And once you have given yourself over to him, do everything you can to prepare yourself to go.

Be prepared

Joshua was scared, but prepared! Joshua learnt from Moses. He learnt the importance of keeping close to God so that when God was ready to use him, as much as he was frightened out of his mind, he had at least started to prepare himself for this new work. This is what the Lord said to him in Joshua 1:9, 'Have I not commanded you? Be strong and courageous. Do not be terrified; do not be discouraged, for the Lord your God will be with you wherever you go.'

So God says to us *go*! We need to learn to obey his commands, don't we? The Lord has said he won't leave us on our own to battle it out. He won't ask us to do something that's impossible. We may feel scared, but we have to be prepared to give it our best shot!

In this book we have talked about witnessing, and about your calling, but there will come a time when you will be ready and able to lead someone to Jesus yourself. For this purpose we have included a chapter on how to lead someone to Christ. These are all subjects that can really help you to grow as a Christian, so take time out to go over those chapters a few times.

Your responsibility is the same as mine, but that doesn't mean God will use you in the same way. When John made himself available to God, he had no idea what he was letting himself in for. But one thing we know—it will be better, greater and more exciting than you ever thought possible. You can make a big impact for the kingdom of God right where you are. Think about it!

3

Life in All Its Dullness

Yes, well, sometimes to look at some people you'd think *that* is what the Lord came to give: 'I come to give you life! But life in all its dullness!' Of course, the real verse says 'fullness', which puts a slightly different slant on things. In this chapter, we'd like to look at ways in which you can have a real full Christian life.

We've all met them, haven't we? Those people who beam all the time and nothing ever gets them down. Annoying, aren't they? But what we are talking about here, is not people who can put on a good act at church or when there are Christians about, but people who really have found the secret of the abundant Christian life.

Changing the subject slightly, have you ever been in a car with a madman? I mean, someone who drives like a complete idiot. There's nothing worse than being offered a lift by some quite innocent-looking person at church, to find out that when they get behind the wheel they have a touch of the Jekyll and Hyde about them! And always, always, they have a sticker in their back window with some really sincere Christian message on like: 'Honk if you love the Lord!' Everyone is hooting and honking like crazy because this guy is breaking every existing speed limit, and he, of course, is waving at everyone thinking, 'I didn't know there were so many Christians around!'

Over the top? I don't think so. And, let's face it, ministers are often the worst!

Chariots of fire

In 2 Kings 9:14–29 there's a great story about someone named Jehu.

Jehu was on his way to see King Joram (I'm sorry but I don't make these names up) in his chariot and was in a bit of a hurry. Now there was a lookout at King Joram's place and he was up in a tower and he spotted Jehu and his men coming towards them. At that distance it was hard to tell who these troops belonged to, so in true cartoon style he yelled out, 'I see some troops coming!' Obviously the king was rather upset about this and sent out a messenger to find out why these troops were heading his way. Unfortunately for him, when the messenger reached Jehu, Jehu demanded that he joined them and so the message never got back to the king. This happened a few times, and the king began to get a bit frustrated trying to find out who was heading his way. Then the lookout came to his rescue, 'It's OK,' he said. 'I can't see his face, but I can recognize his driving. It's got to be Jehu, because he's driving like a madman!'

2 Kings 9:20 does actually state that Jehu drove like a madman! But, you see, this was how things were with Jehu. Whenever God asked him to do something, he did it furiously! There was no second best with Jehu. When the Lord asked him to kill Ahab's family, he absolutely slaughtered anyone to do with them. He really went to town when following the Lord's instructions.

That might all sound a little gory, but we need to have the same fire and zeal for the things God asks us to do. That kind of passion is rare today. The Christian church is often half-hearted and a bit too comfy. We like to enjoy our life, take things easy and do a little good now and again when it suits us. Words like 'challenge', 'adventure' and 'excitement' are rare in the Christian life.

Fire from heaven

Turn further back in Kings and look at 1 Kings 18:16–46 and you get the tale of Elijah and the prophets of Baal. Now here was a real challenge: two altars built and two bulls slaughtered, plenty of wood for the fire for the sacrifice...but no fire. The challenge of this 'contest' was for the prophets of Baal to call on their god to light the fire on their altar, and then for Elijah to call on the living God to do the same for his.

Elijah had such confidence in God, that he really mocked the other lot to death. As they were screaming their heads off to a non-existent god, Elijah was yelling out, 'Give it a bit more welly. Perhaps he's asleep, this god of yours!' Boy, you have to be confident in your own God to give out this kind of abuse!

Anyway, the prophets went on yelling and screaming and cutting themselves with spears and chucking complete wobblies all over the place. They must have been exhausted! By this time Elijah is probably getting bored with it all and decides that it's time to call on the real God and get things warmed up a bit. But rather than just saying, 'OK, you guys, this is how it's done,' he commands the people to go and fetch four large jars of water. Having done this, he then proceeds to pour the water over the altar he wants God to set fire to. (Challenging, eh?) Not satisfied with this, he gets them to do it over and over again until the trench round the altar starts to resemble a moat.

There's nothing that says Elijah then started screaming and cutting himself. It just says Elijah prayed, 'Lord...let it be known today that you are God in Israel and that I am your servant' (1 Kings 18:36–37). And that was it! Fire everywhere! On the altar, the sacrifice, the wood, the stone, the soil and then even the trench!

Sitting on the fence

Elijah had challenged the people earlier with these words: 'How long will you waver between two opinions? If the Lord is God, follow him, but if Baal is God, follow him.' That statement is followed by some very cutting words: 'But the people said nothing' (1 Kings 18:21).

I think this is the situation we find ourselves in. If Jesus is Lord then give him your best. If you don't think he is, then stop playing about. With Christ it's all or nothing.

Life with adventure, challenge and excitement can be ours, but it means following Jesus 100% and not playing about. Christians are not meant to have ordinary lives, but extraordinary lives! Life in all its fullness! That's what it was like in Acts, wasn't it? They didn't live out a cold, dry religion, rather they lived out an experience of Jesus in their lives. Luke says in Acts 4 that great grace and power was on them all. Not just a chosen few, but all of them. Because more than anything they wanted to work out God's will in their lives.

You see we have two problems. One is that we are too scared to find out what God really wants for our lives, and then two, when we do find out, we are too afraid to take the initial step to activate it!

It's a crying shame that God wants us to have an

abundant and extraordinary life, and we just won't put our minds to it. Where would Elijah have been if he hadn't been confident of his God? You see, we can be more like Christ—we can live life in all its fullness—it just takes two steps, one down and one up. Are you ready?

The step down

Let me tell you a sad tale about a young man who came out of Bible college as green as the Welsh valleys he came from (well, he was from Cardiff, anyway), and how he was sent to his first church in the East End of London. Oh, all right then, I'll come clean, this is actually a story about John and his search for abundant life. I always find that real life stories put the point over better, don't you? Anyway, as I said, John had just come out of Bible college and had already prayed, 'Lord, anywhere but London.' What he didn't realize, of course, was that he had to come to London to fall in love with me—but that's another story!

So here was John, born into a Christian family and not at all ready for the East End and the Tibbs brothers (who incidentally blew up a cafe near his home on his first week in the area!). Still, mustn't grumble, so John put on a brave face and went to look for a flat on his minister's salary of nine pounds a week. Flats in London at the time were around thirty pounds a week, and he soon found himself in a flat so grotty that the woman nearly paid *him* to take it! The local Christians were very generous and began to give John all the kinds of things that a bachelor needs to keep alive: sauce-pans, knives and forks, chairs and...a frying pan!

As you will no doubt realize, fellas living on their own only know how to fry or grill things. (If you'd like to prove me wrong on this point, both John and myself are open to dinner invitations!) So the frying pan was

gratefully received; it was just that, well, you know that
you get these non-stick frying pans? Well, this was a
'stick' frying pan and John was just about to use it to
cook himself some sausages. Actually, to give you the
full-blown menu, he was going to have sausage and
chips followed by sliced up bananas and custard.
Pretty adventurous stuff for him, but he was quite
confident—that is, until he met the 'stick' frying pan.

John had been in the kitchen for a while, happily
chopping up chips and praising the Lord for the
abundant life he had for him. He had been praying
over the last few days, asking the Lord to teach him
what abundant living was all about so things were
jogging along nicely. Or they were until he put the
sausages into the frying pan. In his own words: 'They
just broke open and became part of the pan. It was
awful. They just continued to spread until they covered
the bottom.'

By now John was a little bit upset and his chips
weren't doing too well either. You see, he had forgotten
them and they were rapidly turning brown! Naturally,
while he was trying to save the charred remains of the
chips, the sausages were getting incredibly well done
on one side, while remaining raw on the other! So
scraping both onto a plate which he threw under the
grill to keep warm, he set about making the custard for
the bananas. Once again in John's own words:
'Anyone can make custard, it's dead easy. So why did I
just get milk and yellow lumps?'

Why indeed? By now he was totally frustrated and
sat at the table staring down at the charcoalled dinner
and the lumpy afters. Then he looked up and said, 'I'm
sorry, Lord, I can't give thanks for this. I'm not thankful
for it, it's a mess.'

Straight away he could hear a sneering voice in his
ear saying: 'And where's your abundant life now? Is

that all it takes, just a burnt dinner and your abundant life goes out of the window!' The devil is crafty, you know. He hits you when you're down and you don't even realize he's doing it!

Happily, John woke up to this fact and realized that he had let the devil get in on the act and so decided it was time to shame him. He said grace and the lesson was learnt. He poured the custard away and made himself some more. It was ace! Not a lump in sight, just beautifully smooth custard!

John had to step down. He had to acknowledge that he had let things get in the way of his Christian life. It wasn't just the cooking going wrong. This had simply made him realize that we have to be prepared to let go of anything in our lives that is hindering our walk with God. We need to deal with the sinful side of our nature so that the abundant life can shine through. Jesus took upon himself our sinful nature for that very reason. 2 Corinthians talks about us being a new creation. Sure, we have the same personality, but the badness has taken a killer blow. The way of the Christian is the way of the cross. God's method for living life in all its fullness is for us to die to our own self rule, or our ego if you like, and that is the *step down*.

The step up

As with baptism, you die to the sin and then rise to the new life, so as we start to associate ourselves with Jesus' death, then Jesus starts to associate his abundant life with us. When Jesus walked on this earth, people were attracted to him, and it can be the same for us, because he said we would do even greater things than he did himself. So once we have died with Christ we can be raised for that new life. Jesus was never noted for the things he didn't do. He was noted for the things he did do. The fruit of the Spirit in our lives is what is going to help us live life in all its fullness.

A while ago, John was studying the fruit of the Spirit and trying to apply them first to Jesus' life and then to his own, and found the easiest way to understand what the fruits of the Spirit were really all about, was to rewrite Galatians 5:22–23 in his own words. You might like to have a go at this yourself.

'Jesus had a deep concern for people; a deep smile that said, "Everything's going to be all right," a deep sense of ease. He didn't want to rush everything. He shared what he had with the needy. He was always helpful. He stood by people in difficulty. He was nice to people and he didn't let his emotions dominate his personality.'

A tall order when you start applying those things to yourself, but it is the way of abundant living. It's open to anyone who has been crucified with Christ. We have the potential to change the world. We have the power, and God is throwing out the challenge, the adventure and the excitement. The choice is yours: drift along or passionately follow. Are you hot or lukewarm? What do you want to do? Enjoy God's best...or endure Christianity's worst?

4

Don't Shut the Door!

A lot of these chapters make you see yourself as other people would see you. This is a good exercise—one that's not done very often.

Through the eyes of an outsider

I wonder what a Christian really looks like to the bloke in the street? And, come to think of it, church must seem ultra-odd! When we go to church we sing differently from the way we do in the bath, and we pray in holy voices rather than the friendly voice we use when we are talking to a familiar face. We put on clothes that are never used during the rest of the week and we say things that we never say during the rest of the week either. And yet we expect the outsider to feel at home. What happened to that nice Mr Bloggs who asked Mr Outsider along to his church? I mean, in the office he came across as quite a stable sort of bloke and now he's whispering and smiling inanely at everyone! He was even hugging another man just now! What's going on?

I'll tell you what's going on—we are shutting the kingdom of God in men's faces. That's what's going on.

Shutting the door

Somehow we have got to start to learn from examples of others, good and bad. Take the Pharisees (Mt 6:1–18). All their emphasis went on what they *did* rather than what they *were*. You know the sort of thing, they liked to pray on street corners so that everyone could see them, and they would boast about how many times a day they prayed and how much money they had given away.

Then, as a special treat, they would make a meal of the fact that they hadn't eaten anything for a week because they were fasting.

What an attractive way to bring people to God. 'Come to the Lord! Pray ninety-five times a day, give all your money away and don't eat. You'll love it!'

Who can blame the outsider for thinking, 'Well, if that's Christianity, I'm not even sure I'm going to like heaven anyway'? This way we are turning people off Jesus, and as we said in previous chapters, it's our responsibility to go into all the world with the gospel.

Separation

When I was at school, one of my favourite lessons was Domestic Science (cookery and things). Not because I was particularly good at it, more because it was one of those lessons where you are allowed to talk and work at the same time. Mind you, our teacher taught us some pretty nifty tricks and one of the ones I still enjoy doing is separating the yolk of an egg from the yucky bit. If you haven't had this experience, you don't know what you're missing! All you have to do is break the egg shell very carefully and hold all of the egg in one half of the shell. (Why don't you try it?) Then you have to try and drop the yellow bit into the empty half of the shell, by letting the sharp edge of the shell cut across the white bits. (Still with me?) Now, you have to do this several times before all the yellow is in one half and all the white is in the other. If you're anything like me, nine times out of ten you will pierce the yellow and it will run into the white and make an 'orrible mess.

You know what I'm going to say, don't you?

Yes! A perfect example of separation. Both the white and the yellow belong to the egg, but they are clearly different, and when one merges with the other we get a cloudy mish-mash of both. In the same way Christians and non-Christians belong to the same world and should therefore get along side by side, even though there is a difference. However, once we try to mix the two, we are in trouble. We can't distinguish who's who and it all begins to look the same.

Jesus sent us into the world, and so we dare not lose touch with those who live in the same world as we do (Jn 17:11, 14–15, 18). Jesus understood the dilemma that brought on us. It's no joke trying to be separate and at the same time part of the world.

How is it done?

The problem is, if we conform to other people's ideas and standards, then people won't be able to see Jesus in us. On the other hand, if we isolate ourselves it makes anything we have of Jesus useless to those who need it! In Matthew it talks about the fact that it's no good lighting a lamp and then hiding it under a bowl or something, because no one's going to see it (Mt 5:15).

So how do we do it? Well, Jesus said, 'As [the Father] sent me into the world I have sent them' (Jn 17:18). I don't know if we dare look at how the Father sent Jesus into our world. He was vulnerable, exposed, open to temptation. He was sent into a hazardous world where the enemy was seeking to destroy him (1 Pet 5:8). There is danger involved in jumping into the world at the deep end, but there again there's danger in lots of things. There's danger involved in sending a child to school all alone without a parent, but unless he is, he will never mature and grow.

We all know what happens to an over-protected child. The minute a problem arises he just can't cope. The child can grow up to be unbalanced and usually disobedient. If we allow that to happen in the Christian life we will have a world full of unbalanced and disobedient Christians. To withdraw from the world is bad news and yet many Christians don't even have non-Christian friends. If that is so, it also means the voice of Christ won't be heard because we have withdrawn from the very people Jesus sent us to talk to! And when you think about it, if you have no unsaved friends, how on earth are you going to understand how people think and feel? That's why this chapter is designed to make you look at Christians from the world's point of view! It is impossible to communicate with the ordinary bloke in the street if you don't know the first thing about his feelings. So it is done by letting your light shine!

Light v darkness

Jesus fully expects us to let the world know he lives. Matthew 5:16 says, 'Let your light shine before men, that they may see your good deeds and praise your Father in heaven.' Switching on a light does incredible things—it doesn't matter how dark it is. You've seen loads of films, I expect, where someone goes down into a cave and everything gets mega-dark, and because it's a film nobody has a torch that works. Then suddenly some little kid comes running up with a box of matches and with just one little match he manages to light up the whole film set! Maybe a bit far fetched, but one little match can make a whole lot of difference in the dark.

Jesus said we must be salt and light. So what does salt do? Salt preserves food. If you rub salt into meat it will keep fresh for ages, but if you leave meat on its own for a while it will soon start walking away by itself. (If you've never had this experience, come round to our house when we've been away on tour and left some in the fridge!)

So if your office is a bad place to work or your school is a rotten place to be, then it's because the salt isn't out there getting rubbed into the meat. If you know you are a mature Christian then for goodness' sake get out there and mix with these people—stop them going rotten. You can do it. If you want to be an effective counsellor then it's time to stop shouting at people from a distance and get close to them. Dare I say it? Get involved! God does not want us to remove ourselves from the people, but he does ask for a heart that is totally his. So if you want to set something apart for Jesus, makes sure it's your heart—not your presence from the world.

Back to practicalities

OK, you're doing great so far. Now let's put a few A-B-C's down.

a) Don't be nervous

You may feel a little nervous, but this is a fact: the non-Christian is tons more nervous than you because you are presenting him with facts that he has ignored or hidden away from all his life. Things like sin, death and judgement.

b) Accept people as they are

Anyone can like nice people, but we are asked to love the unlovely as well. We need to care for everyone and gently lead them away from the things that are destroying their lives and point them to Jesus who can give them the best life ever.

c) Take the initiative

It's so easy to go to a Christian concert or something and just say hello to your mates. No one likes to step forward and start chatting to someone they've never met before, but it's something we need to do if we are going to start building bridges into people's lives. How are we going to get to know someone unless we talk to them?

In Luke 14:12–13 it talks about people who were invited to a feast, and none of them had anything much to offer in return. Some were poor, some crippled. It's awful to realize, but we prefer to talk to people who we can get something out of. Oh yes we do! We readily come up with, 'Oh, he's a personal friend of mine,' if the conversation turns to some prominent member of society. But we're not quite so quick to identify with the bloke on the dole with tattoos up his arm and an ultra-noticeable beer gut!

Christians must be hospitable (not sympathetic or patronizing). We must go out of our way when things are just not convenient, and get out of our normal circle of friends for the sake of God's kingdom. The Lord told us to go. He didn't say, 'Just sit there and I'll bring them to you.'

d) Be adaptable (1 Cor 9:19–27)

Don't expect the non-Christian to fall in line with your ideals and standards, or your way of talking and thinking. Just because you feel terribly righteous, you shouldn't expect the non-Christian to change to your mode of life.

I always felt it was a shame that when we were working in the East End of London, cockneys would become Christians and almost immediately move out of the area!

You watch *EastEnders*, don't you? Well, could you imagine if Lofty, Angie and Ethel all became Christians as part of the story . . . and then all moved out of Albert Square! You'd be screaming for the story to make them stay where they were and influence the other characters. You wouldn't want Angie to lose that fabulous smile and character and turn into an uninteresting, unassuming, plodding type of person, would you? I'm sure you would want to see her use those dazzling, winning ways on the customers at the Queen Vic—but for Jesus this time!

And yet time and time again, we expect people to take on our personality—because it suits us. But it's wrong. The Lord says, 'Follow my example, go into the world as the Father sent me.' So how did Jesus go into the world? Look at Philippians 2:7–8. Yes! He put aside the glory and his reputation! What people thought of Jesus was of no consequence to him. He let his reputation lie in tatters. But us? Well, our reputation is pretty precious—especially among other Christians —and often we find that what some Christians think of us is in fact more important than what the Lord thinks of us.

When Jesus entered our world, he was tempted in the same ways that we are tempted, but he didn't give in to it. He never sinned. He lived like we live, he shared our lifestyle and lived in the same world as us—only he stopped short of sinning. We would never have understood what God was like if he hadn't sent his Son to show us, would we?

So how can you expect a non-Christian to understand what being a Christian is all about, if your life doesn't show him? We must be adaptable; get alongside people just like Jesus did.

Your life is a picture of what the non-Christian is to expect. Do you think it's something he would want? Or are you still shutting the kingdom of God in his face?

5

'I Want to Become a Christian'

Those fatal words! No, I know they shouldn't be, but after all the witnessing and counselling you can go through with people, it's still a bit of a mind-blower when they come up and say, 'OK, I'm convinced. Now what do I do?' And have you noticed how people manage to catch you at the most awkward time possible?

I remember a group called Heartbeat saying that they had been in school all day taking lessons, and they had just packed everything into their van. As they began to pull out of the driveway, they were waved down by a pupil. Thinking that it was a girl autograph-hunting, one of them put her head out of the window to say hello. And then it happened! 'I want to become a Christian!'

It's so exasperating and in your mind you can imagine a Basil Fawlty voice saying, 'What's the matter with you? We've been in your school all day. Wasn't there enough time during lunch to talk to us? I mean, does it *have* to be now? Can't it wait until we're halfway down the road? That would be much more inconvenient!'

But, of course, Heartbeat were very gracious and spent time with their heads hanging out of the van window, leading the young lady to the Lord.

At a Christian holiday called 'Royal Week' we were taking all the posters and things down as we were finished for another year. There were kids everywhere trying to cadge posters that we didn't want and helping to untie things from the rafters of the barn. There must have been two or three ghetto blasters playing different cassettes and people coming up every five minutes with their parents to say a tearful goodbye. And it was among all this confusion that two girls came up to me.

The first girl explained that her friend wanted to become a Christian and she couldn't find anyone for her to talk to. So I smiled and said, 'OK, meet me in the caravan in fifteen minutes.' They both looked very worried and said, 'Couldn't you do it now?' I was standing there with a staple gun in one hand and half a ton of rubbish in the other feeling very unprepared, but they seemed so anxious that I said, 'OK,' and went through with both of them (it's always just as well to talk to them both . . . you never know . . .) why Jesus died and their responsibility. After only five minutes, the young girl was happily crying and looking terribly relieved, so I said, 'Look, the best thing you can do now is to run round the camp and let off a bit of steam.'

'Oh, I can't do that!' she replied, 'I'm going home!' And with that she got into a waiting car and was driven off the campsite! I was so surprised. I know she said 'now', but I didn't realize quite how urgent the situation was!

Then there was the occasion while I was working part time in a male boutique. One of the guys there was for ever asking questions about my faith. He wasn't trying to be stroppy, he simply wanted to understand why it meant so much to me. One day we were making a coffee in the downstairs 'Jeans and Trousers' department when he said, 'OK, I'm convinced. What do I have to do to become a Christian?' Taking my cue, I explained that he had to pray and ask the Lord to forgive him and ask Jesus to come into his life. 'All right,' he said, 'but you'll have to say the words and I'll repeat them.'

'What now?' I cried. 'You cannot be serious! We are in a shop with a potential customer arriving any second!' He looked a little surprised and then explained to me that if I thought that belonging to Jesus was the ultimately most important thing in the world, then surely now was the best time. And as that is what the Scripture says as well, I was a little bit loathe to argue with him. But it was so awkward praying with one eye open in case anyone came in!

So there we are, it seems to be just the way it goes. When people say they'd like to become Christians they usually mean that minute.

Yes please!

Supposing you are confronted with a willing convert and need to try and say all the right things, here are some words of advice. Don't say too much or too little. If we are not careful we can drive people away with our enthusiasm, but usually the boot is on the other foot, isn't it? Remember, you are not expected to be able to deliver the whole of the gospel in one go. I'm sure you found out for yourself that understanding all God has for you takes a long time and you don't expect to take it all in the moment you get saved. Pray silently to the Lord for the right words. You may think you don't know what to say, but look at the woman from Samaria. All she said to her friends was, 'Come and see a man who told me everything I ever did! Could this be the Christ?'

Andrew went flying to his brother Simon Peter

yelling, 'We have found the one Moses spoke about...
Jesus of Nazareth!'

We always try to complicate things and yet simple
words are the most effective. It's really important that
we be ourselves, be real and show our love for Jesus
and each other.

People who want to become Christians will differ in
how much they already know about the Lord. Some
will have been listening to Christians for ages; some
will hardly know much more than his name. So you
need to make the gospel as simple as possible. There
are various ways of doing this, but I think that these
diagrams relating to The Bridge to Life are very effective.

Got a pencil?

Draw the following diagram on a scrap of paper.

MAN   SIN   GOD

Then explain that ever since Adam sinned, man has been separated from God. The huge gulf between God and man was caused directly by sin, and it still is today.

Now draw the next diagram:

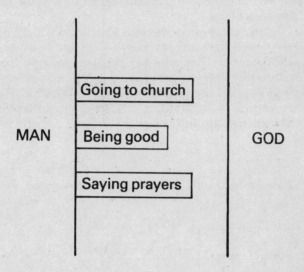

Explain how people try to span that gulf with things they hope God will like. Ask the person you are talking to for ideas of his own. There may well be ways he has tried to get to God himself and perhaps you could share ways you used to have.

Go on to talk about the fact that none of these things were good enough and God couldn't even look at them. Read up on Hebrews 9 and 10 beforehand so that you can explain how God used to require the blood of an innocent animal to be shed to cover the people's sins, and that this had to happen every year to be of any use (Heb 10:3–4).

Then explain how Jesus came into the world to be

used as the perfect once-and-for-all sacrifice. Draw the next diagram:

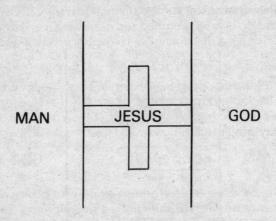

Explain how Jesus is the only way to God.

Important verses

There are many verses to help you show this person what he has to do to give his heart to the Lord. We'll go through them:

The fact of sin (Rom 3:23)

'For all have sinned and fall short of the glory of God.' Show him this verse to help him realize that there are no exceptions to the rule. That's why nothing else would fill the gap.

Penalty of sin (Rom 6:23)

'For the wages of sin is death, but the gift of God is eternal life.' Once this person has realized that he has sinned, he will then be able to acknowledge this verse.

Penalty paid by Christ (Rom 5:8)

'But God demonstrates his own love for us in this: While we were still sinners, Christ died for us.' Given the fact that we have sinned and deserve to die, we now read that Jesus died for us even though we were sinners.

Salvation is a free gift (Eph 2:8–9)

'For it is by grace you have been saved, through faith— and this not from yourselves, it is the gift of God—not by works, so that no-one can boast.' We don't have to do anything to earn heaven. In fact there is nothing we *can* do!

Receive it (Jn 1:12)

'Yet to all who received him, to those who believed in his name, he gave the right to become children of God.' It is more than an acknowledgement, we need to receive this gift from God and claim it as our own.

Be assured (1 Jn 5:11–12)

'And this is the testimony: God has given us eternal life, and this life is in his Son. He who has the Son has life; he who does not have the Son of God does not have life.' Once you have received Jesus into your life, the Bible assures you that you are indeed a child of God and fit for his kingdom!

It doesn't matter how many times you read about or go over the reason behind God's great plan for saving the human race, it's still tremendously exciting. Try to go over these things in your mind and on paper whenever you can, because it is so much better to be able to explain these things clearly. Most questions that you will be asked are covered either in the diagrams or in the verses I've just given you. It's also wise to have a copy of some good leaflets like *Journey into Life* and *Coming Home* because you don't know who is going to ask you these questions or when.

So, what happens next?

6

Looking After New Christians

I know it shouldn't be, but this is a constant headache to the church, so let's face the problem where we can see it. Everyone has different ideas about what should happen to a new convert. I have heard a well-known evangelist say that once someone has accepted Jesus into his life, then he should just get on with it. I can't really agree with that, although I realize that in theory, once you have become a Christian, you have a new life and the Lord is there to help you through any trials.

But surely it's going to help if we help? So how should we look after new converts? How much is their responsibility and how much is ours?

The aim

In other chapters we have talked about witnessing and how we go on and on about the great choruses we sing in church and how friendly the people are, and yet the most important thing for a new Christian is getting a grasp on who Jesus is. Once they get to know Jesus then all the other stuff becomes relevant. Before that happens it's just music and words. We really must get to grips

with the fact that a new Christian (most times) is
unaware of the greatness of the gospel and won't really
understand for ages exactly why Jesus died. When you
think how people go to Bible colleges and study loads
of books on the subject, it's hardly surprising that you
can't take it all in on the first day.

New Christians are like new-born babies. The Bible
says they are and so we must treat them accordingly.
We must not expect them to 'behave' like Christians. A
new Christian might still swear and laugh at rude
jokes. There again, a new baby dribbles and wets his
nappy. Neither things are particularly cute, but they
are part of growing up. Eventually the child will be
potty-trained and will grow his own teeth—just like
the Christian will grow up and learn from the Lord
(with a little bit of help from you). We read quite a lot in
our newspapers about abandoned babies. They die if
they are not found within hours, because a newly-born
baby cannot fend for himself, he needs all the help he
can get.

There are two very important questions for the new
Christian to learn the answers to:

Who is Jesus?

In an earlier counselling situation we will no doubt
have mentioned that Jesus is the way to God. He was
the one that spanned the gulf in our drawing. Without
him we would still have been trying to get to God by
our own efforts and never making it. Once it is understood who Jesus is, then the answers to a lot of questions fall into place. Spend time going over and over why
Jesus died so that your new convert gets to see how
incredibly important Jesus is.

What does Jesus want of me?

This question cannot be answered until your convert

has acknowledged the first question. Where people do not acknowledge Jesus is God, you will find they won't take Christianity any further. But once they *do*, then the next question is imperative. It's quite something to all of a sudden wake up to the fact that Christianity is not just a ticket to heaven, but a responsibility to the rest of the world. Once you believe the truth about Christ, you must not only believe it, but stake your life on it! And that's where a lot of people chicken out.

Growing Christians should constantly ask themselves the above questions as they seek to learn more about the Lord they follow.

The three factors

If we split follow-up into three factors we can clearly work out what we should be doing. These are: the Christian, the Scriptures, and the Holy Spirit. Each has a part to play.

The Christian

This is your part. The Christian's role in follow-up is summed up in 1 John 1:1–3.

> That which was from the beginning, which we have heard, which we have seen with our eyes, which we have looked at and our hands have touched—this we proclaim concerning the Word of life. The life appeared; we have seen it and testify to it, and we proclaim to you the eternal life, which was with the Father and has appeared to us. We proclaim to you what we have seen and heard, so that you also may have fellowship with us. And our fellowship is with the Father and with his Son, Jesus Christ. We write this to make our joy complete.

The Christian's role is to pass on the great things that God has done in his life. You need to be able to sit and

chat over a cup of coffee about the things that have
happened in your life which have made being a Christian so worth while.

The Scriptures

I remember taking a new Christian along to an after-
church meeting at someone's house and we sat around
on the floor and began to sing a few choruses. The new
guy stopped us and said, 'Look, I read something in the
Bible yesterday and it was really great. Can we stop
singing and read it?' 'It' turned out to be James—all of
it. You see, this guy had heard singing before, but he
had never read the Bible as a living book and he was so
excited, he wanted to read it again! We ended up
having a really good time discussing the themes that
James had brought out and to this new Christian it was
poetry!

Scripture is just another way of answering the
question 'Who is Jesus?' and it answers it so well! And
because it's so important for new converts to get in to
the Bible, we need to start 'nurture groups'—or whatever you'd like to call them. (They always sound like
something that happens in a garden centre to me.) But,
seriously, we need to find a nice place where we can get
together with new Christians and just one or two older
Christians. I suppose the most obvious place would be
someone's front room, but you may have better ideas
than that.

To do your job well, you need to become a part of that
person's life. You need to study the Scriptures with
them and go and support them when they are playing
for the local football team. Yes! You! It's not enough to
be their spiritual leader, you should be out there being
a friend as well. So following up a new convert is going
to cost you quite a bit. You will have to work out a plan
so that you're there when you're needed. It is a lot of

hard work and unfortunately that's why many missions fail. People can't be bothered with follow-up, but show me a church that has its follow-up sorted out, and I'll show you a healthy growing church!

One other word on being a friend: Proverbs 25:17. I'm not going to tell you what it says, I think you should look it up for yourselves, and take heed.

The Holy Spirit

The Holy Spirit does the convincing. He brings home the truth of the Scriptures to an individual's life. *Give him time to work*! We are always in such a hurry to see results. I think it's just the way the world is now. All the adverts on TV are guaranteeing immediate results with their products: 'Buy this product and you'll never have spots again!' 'Wipe this new polish on your furniture and your table will immediately look like you've just bought it!' We live in a very 'now' age. But when it comes to the work of the Holy Spirit, we have to learn to let go.

The Holy Spirit takes things a step at a time with people, while we tend to want to rush them. God deals with us as individuals because that's what we are—we all do things at different paces. There is a time for us to do our work and a time for the Holy Spirit to do his, and we shouldn't try to do it for him.

Again we can go back to the illustration of bringing up a child. There's nothing more frustrating than watching a child try to walk on his own, or try to put those funny-shaped bricks into funny-shaped holes. It makes you want to reach out and help. You so desperately want to say, 'No, look, that one goes with that one!' or, 'Hold my hand and I'll help you to walk across the room.'

There are times when we watch our new converts go from bad to worse and we think they are never going to make it. They struggle and wrestle with God and it's so hard to stand by and watch them do it, but this is when they need us as a friend rather than a guide. The Holy Spirit is at work and right now they need us to pat them on the back and cheer them forward, rather than to sit them down and give them some deep counselling.

We are the ones who introduce people to Jesus, but he saves them and brings about that new birth. We can't do the work of the Holy Spirit for him and we can't do the work of the Scriptures either. But all three aspects are needed for healthy follow-up.

Pray

This is most important. Spend time with your new Christians talking to the Lord together. Make it natural. Let him realize that God understands his prayers however they are prayed. Prayer times should be absorbing times spent in laughter, tears and confidence.

The harvest

We'll bring this chapter to an end with a challenge.

> Jesus went through all the towns and villages, teaching in their synagogues, preaching the good news of the kingdom and healing every kind of disease and sickness. When he saw the crowds, he had compassion on them, because they were harassed and helpless, like sheep without a shepherd. Then he said to his disciples, 'The harvest is plentiful but the workers are few. Ask the Lord of the harvest, therefore, to send out workers into his harvest field.' (Mt 9:35–38).

There are plenty of harassed and helpless people around you and you have the answer.

7

That Horrid Age

We are always being asked about young teens. I suppose that's because it's one of the age groups we deal with rather a lot. At least a couple of times a year we are left in charge of hundreds and hundreds of them, and they all seem to have a great time. I know loads of people have written books on 'understanding teenagers', but this chapter isn't an in-depth psychological study on their behaviour, it simply aims to help you treat them like human beings!

You must be able to remember being thirteen (unless you haven't been there yet). It was probably one of the most horribly lovely years of your life. As we visit school after school, we generally find that the early teens are the biggest problem. The trouble is, when you're thirteen you are not old enough to do anything, and too old to do anything else! You don't know whether you're supposed to be an adult or a child, whether you should be skipping with a rope or eyeing up the talent. You suffer endlessly from remarks like, 'You can't go to the disco on your own. It's late, your dad will have to walk there with you.' Then on the other side of the scale: 'I know it's dark, but it's only

eight o'clock. Surely you can go down to the corner
shop by yourself?'

When we take lessons with young teens, they are
invariably caught up in the adult versus child thing.
We ask them if they have any questions they'd like to
ask, and they either come up with, 'Where did you buy
your jeans?' or, 'What about the third world?' Or even,
'What's your favourite colour?' And which ever
question they ask, they are going to get some comeback
from other kids in the class. If they ask about your
favourite colour, people are going to say, 'How
childish!' On the other hand, if they dare to ask about
the problems of the starving millions, then their friends
look embarrassed and say, 'Oh, Tracey, *really*!' as
though Tracey had a real bad case of showing off! You
can't win when you are a young teen. It's impossible!

So now, can you imagine how difficult it is for young
teens in church? This is the ideal age for kids to drop
church. When they are being teased mercilessly for
everything from boyfriends to spots they just don't
need to be teased about being seen going to church.
This means the church has an incredibly hard time
keeping them.

If the teenager has been brought up in a Christian
home, then there is a chance he will stay with the
church. If he has a non-Christian background, he will
probably leave. Those that make it through to sixteen
usually stay because by then they have started to be
able to cope with the boredom of it all, and will at least
be able to start picking up a few things from the sermon.
Does that sound brutal? Good! It's absolutely no use
going round with your head in the clouds thinking that
they'll come through, because they desperately need
your help, and to help them you need to understand a
few things.

'Integrating eleven to fourteen year olds' is a seminar

that John and I give at Christian conferences and youth weekends alike, and when put to the test, there are an awful lot of youth leaders who have no interest in the likes and dislikes of the kids they are trying to reach. Now this doesn't mean that you have to become like a kid again, but it would help if you could just take an interest. Happily for you I can't put you to the test at the moment, but on several occasions we have given people a quiz on the interests of young teens and were astounded to see many, many blank pieces of paper at the end of it.

So why can't I put you to the test? Simply because by the time this book is published (even if it were just a gap of two or three months), all the fads and fashions would be out of date! But I will try and give you an example. We asked youth leaders, 'Where do Five Star come from?' Most people came back with, 'Who are Five Star?' We asked, 'Who is Don Johnson?' and people were yelling, 'Never heard of him!' It was fun and a good laugh, but afterwards folk were coming over and saying, 'Boy that was so embarrassing. I could hardly answer anything.' And then they would start to question their own use as a youth leader. Great! We don't want them to stop leading youth, but we *do* want them to have an inkling about the kids they are leading!

OK, let's have a quick look at what eleven to fourteen year olds like (accepting that it is 1987 at the time of writing).

Girls: Reading *Smash Hits* and pulling out the posters in the middle... Listening to or watching Aha... East-Enders... Saturday Superstore... Pop music... Top Shop ... Hair... Make-up... Writing notes... fluffy mascots.

Boys: Computers... Sport—especially soccer... *Miami Vice*... Heavy Metal—or any music with a bit of aggression in it... Musical equipment—especially guitars and synthesizers... anything technical... video games . . . *EastEnders*.

I wonder how many of these things you actually like yourself? John is always telling people that the reason I get on with young teens is that I have the mental age of a twelve year old, so I have no problem discussing things with them! But as I said, although you don't have to be like that, you do need to understand.

Don't you think it would be a great idea if youth leaders went to their young teens and said, 'Look, why don't you all come round to my house on Thursday night and get me to watch *Top of the Pops* with you? I don't know the first thing about it, but I'll ask the questions for a change and you can fill me in on the details!' Wouldn't that be great! I'm sure the kids would love to take their youth leader on this great cultural experience! And it would be good for everyone. The kids wouldn't be expecting the youth leader to particularly *like* what he saw and heard, but at least he would have some idea of their everyday conversation!

If you don't like pop music, you will probably have already lost some of your young people. If you like sport you will relate to a good proportion of the lads. Sit down and think it over—it will make a lot of sense in the end.

How do you treat kids?

Let's start with Christian kids. It is imperative that you treat them as adults. You may find that hard, but if you treat them as kids you'll have a Sunday school picnic on your hands—all the thirteen and fourteen year olds will clear off and leave you with just the eleven and twelve year olds and that's no good for either of you. When teenagers are treated like adults they will respond as near to the real thing as they can! You can't expect them to behave perfectly, but you'll get a lot more sense out of them if you give them responsibilities instead of lectures. They may even start asking to help!

Remember that kids don't have a slapstick sense of humour—that happens when they are older, or younger —and going back to what I said about being embarrassed, it's the wrong age for silly jokes and custard pies. They have enough to put up with.

With non-Christians, again the most important thing is to be adult with them. Be totally genuine. If they do talk about some fashion or music that you know nothing about then it's your turn to be educated! Ask about it, let them see that you want to know, because if you pretend to be on their wavelength when you're not, you will find yourself in very hot water. To get through to young teens you need music, drama, humour and entertainment. These things break down barriers. Any of these things done as professionally as possible, will bring respect from your kids. And once they realize you are being genuine with them, they will start giving you credibility.

I have lost count of the number of times teachers have said to us, 'This class is tough. They hate RE and they'll give you a real hard time.' Honestly, 98% of the time they're soon eating out of your hands and the teacher is sitting in the corner mumbling things like: 'Well, they don't react that way with me...they *ate* the last Christian that came in....' We often find that the big stroppy lads are the first to offer to load the gear into the car for us; the loud-mouths are the ones that ask the best questions and the trendy ones tend to go all shy and whisper questions about my hair extensions and how I get away with it at church. And that's all because when they ask, 'Do you like *EastEnders*?' we can spout on longer than they can about it. And when they ask, 'What was the last LP you bought?' and it's the one everyone else in the class wants, but won't be able to

afford for ages, they will relax and talk about your
Christian faith as naturally as any of the other subjects.
I suppose they don't feel threatened that way.

But of course, kids are different today, aren't they?
You weren't like that in your day, were you? Well,
listen to this:

> Our youth now live in luxury. They have bad manners and
> contempt for authority, they show disrespect for their
> elders and love to chatter in place of exercise. Children are
> now tyrants, not the servants of their households. They no
> longer rise when their elders enter the room. They contra-
> dict their parents, chatter in front of company, gobble their
> food and tyrannize their teachers....

And *that*, my friends, was written by Aristotle! (With
grateful thanks to Grantley Watkins who found it before
me!) There's nothing new under the sun.

The problem at the moment is that kids want Jesus,
but they don't want church. We know full well that we
can bring them to the Lord—we have spent the last
nine years on the road and in and out of over 800
schools proving that point—it's just that there's a
problem putting them in churches afterwards. A lot of
that subject is dealt with in the next chapter.

So what do we give them?

Multi-media, fast-moving programmes, short items,
constant change, involvement, debates, logical
answers. Do yourself a favour and start watching
children's TV. Watch *Saturday Superstore* and
Blockbusters and you'll see they are all fast-moving, and
most of the time there is music being played in the
background. There are loads of things going on at once,
and plenty of ad-lib bits.

If you are going to have debates or discussions on provocative subjects like sex and violence, make sure you have some jolly good answers. *It is not enough* to tell a teenager, 'You must not do that.' They will want to be given a perfectly logical explanation as well. No smart answers please, just common sense and logic. They need to know why things are wrong.

Mix your programme. Along with the discussions and prayer times, have times when you go and dig old folks' gardens, do some fund raising, have marathons. Kids have an incredible amount of surplus energy, even if you haven't, so make use of it!

Kids want life! Reality! Interest! And most important of all, they want Jesus! So don't disappoint them!

8

The Credibility Gap

Is it a good thing to bring today's world into our Christianity? With so much talk about keeping holy and clean and not being in the world and all that, there are many Christians too terrified of living in it—let alone using it for their benefit!

It seems to me there are far, far too many counterfeits of Christianity going on around us at present. Even as I sit here typing this book, I can look across the road and watch over 500 people cramming themselves into our town hall for a celebration session that has gone decidedly wonky, to say the least. We have to put up with people approaching us and saying, 'Hey, you're a Christian, aren't you? Well, what about these people down the road that believe in beating up their kids and throwing all their toys away? Are they the same faith as you?'

And Jehovah's Witnesses are at the door night and day. Try as I might, I can't get them to actually take a copy of *I'm a Christian But...* to read when they get home. The Hare Krishna lot have been round in their usual anoraks (well, it gets cold this time of the year if you're only wearing a flowing robe), giving out sweets to people and trying to stand on the same spot as the Moonies with their potted plants.

What I'm saying is, everybody's doing it! They are all out there with their commercialism, getting in on the act, while we are just sitting around wondering why God isn't flooding our churches with the locals. Surely it's about time we ousted out the counterfeits and looked at ways and means of using the world we live in to communicate?

The Credibility Gap was a subject that John and I took as a seminar at a large youth leaders' conference called 'Brainstormers'. We were rather astonished at the lack of initiative when it came to using our own world/town/culture for the gospel.

Now, I don't know whose fault that is. Certainly we can blame ourselves for being too insular—but I think we could also add to that the years and years of teaching from generations before us who told us that going to the cinema was a sin, that having non-Christian friends was a sin, and that wearing a coloured shirt and tie was a sin! We have been bogged down with all this, and now that a few enterprising Christians have managed to get *The Hiding Place* and the story of Jesus shown at the local ABC, and *The Rock Gospel Show* on the telly we don't know which way to turn.

I know, I can hear a few of you yelling, 'But our church is great!' But, believe me, there will only be a few of you. There are pockets of blessing in the Christian church—and that blessing doesn't belong to any particular denomination—but they are the exception rather than the rule. The rest are dwindling. So that leaves us with a choice. We can either close our eyes and carry on regardless, or we can grab today's culture with both hands and use it for the glory of God.

While at Brainstormers, we asked the youth leaders to write out a list of all the things that happen in their normal Sunday service. (It wouldn't be a bad idea if you did this too!) Then we asked them to tick anything in the list that they thought would be relevant to your average kid in the street.

There was much laughter when they looked at their lists and examined the possibilities. Most of the laughter was of the embarrassed kind, but it certainly got us all thinking. I have compiled a rough outline of what we discovered. Maybe you could check it against the list you have written.

Hymns: Almost a foreign language, with tunes you can't pick up easily.

Notices: Mostly irrelevant, especially if you don't happen to know where 'Joan's house' is or what a 'Celebration' is all about.

Prayer: Not for joining in! Although it might be of interest to an onlooker—if the prayers are plain and understandable.

The sermon: Well, although kids are used to having a teacher talking to them from the front, the teacher normally has a blackboard, posters, books and sometimes a video to help explain things a little clearer.

Choruses: Embarrassing. The average kid doesn't do much singing at home, school or anywhere else for that matter (maybe a football match would be an exception).

Drama: Drama is a good thing, as long as it is well done. (It's a bit like watching TV.)

Testimony: As long as it's short and interesting, it may catch their attention.

Responses: Ah, well, at least the words are in front of them.

Music groups, etc: Yes, good idea, helps to make them feel at home.

The welcoming handshake: Vital! Saying hello and being welcomed receive a good response.

Coffee afterwards: Another social activity that is more

familiar.

So there we are, coffee, hellos, some drama, music and the preacher!

I was very pleased after doing this little survey to meet an evangelist who had just come back from New Zealand. He told me that he went to a monthly youth meeting out there, where around 5,000 kids regularly attend!

That many? How? Well, I don't know if you're ready for the answer, but the organizers asked the Christian kids what kind of meeting they would like and they replied, 'One with no choruses, some five-minute spots of music and drama and an animate preacher!'

It seems that the Christian kids came clean and admitted that choruses (as good as they can be) bore no relevance to the non-Christian friends they wanted to bring to this meeting. It was not a time for worship, as their non-Christian friends obviously couldn't praise a God they didn't particularly believe was there. But they were very happy to have a preacher who could use blackboards, videos, drama and music when necessary to get his point across.

And it worked! It worked wonders! To have 5,000 young people each month is what I call closing the Credibility Gap!

Having discussed what could be used in a church service, the big question was, 'How do we get those in authority to change our service?'

As a youth leader, you should have a voice in your church. Young people can get together and find a convenient time to meet with the minister and discuss their feelings. And it's a fact that anyone under the age of forty was brought up with pop music, which means they are more likely to adapt to different ideas and change. It would probably be a good idea to go to your minister with something on paper, rather than a few airy-fairy ideas. Go with the right attitude and don't be resentful. Your minister has a hard enough job as it is. You *do* have a voice in your church—so find the best way of using it. Remember, though, you don't have to change everything about your church service by tomorrow! Just do bits at a time. Introduce some drama, and don't do anything else new until the drama has been more or less accepted. But keep at it. It's becoming more and more important to adapt.

At the moment the only people the church is getting through to at all are a few middle-class people who already have church connections, and that's all well and good, but meanwhile the masses are being missed.

Most people are working class; most people read the *Mirror* or the *Express*; most people watch TV for hours on end. They wash their cars on Sunday mornings and buy fish and chips for tea once a week. They hire videos by the dozen, go down to the social club or disco on a Saturday night and spend all weekend shopping or supporting their favourite football team.

So where does that leave Christianity?

I am not talking about watering down the gospel at all. I don't intend to have us giving out free sherry glasses with each conversion, but because we are frightened of commercialism, we're not doing any-thing! Surely it is not over the top to tell the gospel in today's language, with today's instruments? Jesus cer-tainly used every modern visual aid. He was for ever saying, 'Look at this! Look over there! Look at these lilies! Look at these wineskins! Let me tell you about this taxman/soldier/prostitute. Watch me break this bread while I tell you something important. . . .'

Maybe you think that we are doing this. OK, let me give you a little test. Get yourself a piece of paper and a pen, and see if you can write down, in around three sentences, why Jesus died. Ah, yes, and I want you to write it down in a language that you feel the ordinary person in the street could understand.

It sounds so simple, but we did this test with around a hundred youth leaders and the majority of them were flummoxed. First of all, they were quite confident that they could do it and tried all sorts of different ways to explain Jesus' death. Then, gradually, they got more wound up about it. A few people read out their answers. (See if you can spot what's wrong with these statements.)

'Jesus died to give us life, love and happiness.'

'Jesus gave me peace in my heart and the confidence that I'll go to heaven when I die.'

'Jesus died to give us power to live an extraordinary life.'

As they were read out, people were saying, 'Yes, but that's not *why* he died. That's what happened *because* he died.' Then gradually quite a few of the people in the room realized that they couldn't write out their sentences, simply because they didn't know why Jesus died! I really admired their honesty in this, and so later we had another meeting where we had time to relate this truth to them. Obviously there are various ways of explaining why Jesus died, but it's certainly crucial that you know!

This is how we explained it: 'In Old Testament times, God demanded that a pure animal was sacrificed to him as a sort of offering to say sorry for the rotten things we had done during the year. Then God decided that if he could find a perfect human being, he could be sacrificed once and for all, and we wouldn't have to go through the ritual every year. He would be satisfied with this one perfect sacrifice. Of course, there was no one around to fit the bill, so God had to become a human being and die for us as he was the only one who was perfect. As a human being, his name was

Jesus...the rest is history!'

The ticket to heaven, the happiness and joy, and all the other things about Jesus come after this explanation. Check out Hebrews and read through the bit about the great High Priest and read it until you understand it.

I used to worry about whether my books kept coming back to the same point of making sure that you know you are a Christian. But after chatting to those youth leaders and getting the response we did, I feel quite happy about telling and retelling that same gospel, because we obviously need to hear it!

9

Schools Work

I'm truly amazed! I've been writing books all this time and it's only just been pointed out to me that I have never really written anything on the subject that is actually one of our main ministries: schools! And it is such an important issue—for reasons you will begin to see as we get going.

The law

Before you even think about doing any schools work, or talking to a teacher about such things, let me point out to you that there are laws that must be kept—some written and some unwritten, but all extremely important if you don't want to close the door for any other Christians going in.

First and foremost, you are not in the school to preach the gospel and win souls for Jesus there and then. That is against the law. You are not allowed to go into a classroom and tell the kids what you think they should do with their lives. You can go in and share your own testimony, the story of what happened to you, but on no account should you suggest that they must all do the same.

Kids are at liberty to ask you anything they like, and therefore if someone asks, 'How do I become a Christian?' you can then freely answer this question (but still be extremely careful... praying and laying on of hands is absolutely *out*). You are going in as an example of what a Christian is—that's part of education, to learn about faith and religion. Don't think for one instant that because a very grinny Christian teacher says it's all right for you to preach in his or her class, that it's OK, because it isn't and I can tell you quite a few instances where the results have been disastrous.

Disaster areas

Sorry to read the riot act, but the fact is that people who go in to a school without knowing these facts have had bad effects on our own ministry.

Like ... the time when we were booked to take thirty-five lessons in one school in the Midlands, and just as we arrived the headmaster had a phone call from a school down the road to say that some Christians had just been into his school and had been waving Bibles about and making appeals in assembly. He then advised our headmaster not to let any of these 'born-again' Christians into his school. *And the whole thirty-five lessons were cancelled!*

Like ... the numerous times where we have been the first Christians to go into a school for five or six years, because the last lot who went in started to pray for people in the classroom. So now, five years later, they are just about ready to take the chance, and after some very stern warnings we are allowed to go in and take a ten-minute assembly.

Like ... the number of schools who won't let *anyone* in now, because someone went through the prayer of commitment in the back of *Journey into Life* with everyone in an assembly.

Like...the communist teacher who insisted on a communist assembly because Christians had been in the day before.

Like...the caretaker who took an assembly and told the kids not to come to school the next day because the world was going to end. Now they're not too keen on having anyone else in either.

Appearance

I suppose it's quite hilarious for me with my brightly-coloured hair and the kind of clothes John and I wear, to be talking about appearance. But, you see, it is vitally important that you do things properly if you want to get asked back. In fact, someone said to me not too long ago that if I could go into school with my hair dyed bright orange and red, *and* get asked back, then I must be doing something right.

A lot of the time, it's not so much what you wear, as whether it's clean and ironed. And the same applies to your hair and general looks. People are much more upset if the local youth worker who comes into a school with us has lank, greasy hair and dirty jeans than any colours of the rainbow I'm wearing in my clean hair!

I know you're saying that Jesus looks at your heart, but the headmaster will not take the same view. First impressions count! Remember you are not only going to be talking to a bunch of teenagers in the classroom. The chances are you will be gracing the staffroom and having polite cups of coffee with Heads of years, Governors and goodness knows who else! All it takes is for one member of the staff to object to having to sit with some 'smelly Christian hippy', for your work to go drastically wrong. Believe me, we are trying to help you here!

Be nice to people. We have been told lots of stories by
teachers who have said, 'Oh, that's nice. You're not like
the last lot.' Apparently, 'the last lot' kept their
conversations to the conditions of the souls of everyone
in the staffroom.

Experience

Yes, well, as they say, how are you going to learn if you
don't start somewhere? We think that in this situation,
the best thing you can do is to be involved in a schools
mission with someone who really does know their way
about. That way you can learn a lot without having to
make too many embarrassing errors yourself. Be prepared to sit and watch and take in, rather than actually
doing anything for a while. Also, of course, I don't
know how old you are, but schools could have changed
immensely since you were last in one, and that in itself
will take a bit of getting used to. For instance, kids
don't sing any more—or very rarely. Assembly is the
time when notices are given and the results of football
matches are announced (and even they are rarely
applauded). The only time there is any kind of religious
input is when you or I arrive. They may well have
someone reading a poem or a 'thought for the day'
about being nice to people, but there's very rarely any
Christian content.

Classes are different too, with quite a lot of emphasis
on getting into groups and discussing things, and the
use of videos and visual aids, rather than a teacher
lecturing from the front. But we will deal with these a
little later on.

Who to approach

If schools work has never been done in your area, then you have to start from the beginning. I hope I can explain this bit without upsetting anyone.

As soon as schools work is mentioned in church, someone will come rushing up to say how many Christian teachers they know of in dozens of different schools all over town. The next thing that happens is that everyone gets excited and starts contacting these teachers before anything has been organized. Now, we would like to try and explain the position that the Christian teacher is in (and if you are a Christian teacher, we hope we've put this correctly).

The Christian teacher has to be at that school every day, whether you are in or not, so it is not surprising to find that he will be rather cagey at times about you coming on to his territory. First of all, he doesn't know what you are going to do in his lessons. Will the kids enjoy it or will they spend the whole lesson ribbing you to bits and jeering you to death? Will the rest of the staff take to you or will it help to make his reputation as a 'religious maniac' stand faster than ever?

The other type of Christian teacher is the type I spoke of earlier, who will let you come in with open arms and do whatever you want regardless of the rules of the school. If it gets him out of a few lessons—then you are welcome! He was thinking of leaving anyway....

Now, in both of these cases, I hope you can see that the best person to go to is the Head of the school. The Head might be a Christian—or he might be the world's greatest atheist—but he will have the interest of his school at heart. If you make an appointment to see him and prepare what you are going to say carefully, then he will listen and give you all the help he can. He will be

fair and unbiased—as long as you are. John and I have
played in hundreds of schools where the Heads have
had no interest in Christianity at all, but they have
been impressed by the professionalism of the music we
play, the way we have conducted the lessons and the
staff's reaction.

Headmasters can arrange for the school hall to be
vacant all day if that's what you need (for music, drama,
activities, etc.), whereas the RE teacher would probably
find himself having to face irate gym teachers if he tried
to organize it himself. Also, a Christian teacher often
wants to keep the Christian worker to himself and
therefore plans a timetable around his own lessons (an
average of twenty-five pupils per lesson) and at the end
of the day you have maybe talked to 150 kids. Again,
the headmaster would want everyone to benefit from
your visit and make arrangements for you to see all of,
say, the second, third and fourth years in the space of
two days!

So, you see, for the sake of the Christian teacher's
peace of mind and in respect for those in higher
authority it is always best to go straight to the top!

Timetable

This is another important aspect. We will talk about
what kind of lessons you can take a little later, but
assuming you have things planned, once again it's very
easy to get over-enthusiastic with the lessons that are
offered to you. Try not to bite off more than you can
chew. You may be offered six lessons in the course of
one day and think that it's a great opportunity, but
when you are giving your testimony or describing the
same illustration for the fourth time without a break,
you'll probably find that all the schoolkids' faces have
merged into one and you can't remember what you

have said to which class! And then, when for the
hundredth time, some kid puts his hand up and says,
'Can you be a Christian without going to church?' you
have to explain it as well as you did in the first lesson,
remembering that this class haven't heard the answer.

So take it easy and do what you know you can cope
with.

What to do

Lessons, as we mentioned earlier, can take many
different forms and you have to find out what you are
good at. For instance, to take a guitar in and sing in a
classroom is not as easy as you maybe imagine. For a
start, your audience is made up of 99% non-Christians
99% of the time. This means you can strike choruses off
your list straight away. Apart from what we have
already explained about kids not singing these days,
there's really not a lot of point in teaching them to sing
praises to a God they couldn't care less about. Therefore,
singing in a classroom has virtually got to be a
performance. You might get them to join in a really
good chorus—but don't bank on it. And if they do,
don't bank on them singing the same words as you! My
mind flashes back to a certain Christian band who tried
to get a hall full of kids to sing, 'We're a bunch of little
'erberts.' Unfortunately, the kids thought it much more
fun to spend the rest of the day singing, 'We're a bunch
of little perverts.'

Always take care to watch for double meanings—
especially in drama sketches.

We were in a classroom once with a Christian who
was telling the class that he knew lots of famous people.
The 'famous' people he knew, however, didn't really
do a lot for the kids, so one fella put his hand up and
asked him if he had ever met Queen. The rest of the

class were sniggering to think of this older guy meeting
a rock band, and to my horror the Christian went on to
explain how he had never actually met Her Royal
Majesty, although she had walked past him once! The
kids were in fits and we had to explain to him why they
were laughing.

If you are going to attempt schools work, it's
important that you have some things in common with
the kids. TV programmes, sport, music, computers, or
whatever—find something that you would both enjoy
talking about and use it as a springboard.

We decided to break this chapter into two and use
the second part to give you some practical ideas for
a school lesson—things you can work on and convert to
your own way of communicating. However, staying
with the lesson for a moment, here are a few more tips.

Avoid red herrings

If you are not careful you can spend an entire lesson
dealing with questions like, 'If Adam and Eve were
white, where did black people come from?' and, 'Do
you believe in UFOs?' Although you can get a good
debate going on these sorts of things, they won't change
anybody's life and you will only go round and round in
circles. We have found that we hardly ever get asked
these sorts of questions, basically because we talk about
ourselves and how we believe our faith helps us in any
number of circumstances. The kids are usually so
wrapped up in asking things like, 'How does God
answer prayers?'; 'Can I pray for a Rolls Royce?'; 'Why
do you sing about Jesus instead of trying to get on *Top
of the Pops*?' and 'What would make you stop believing
in God?' that the 'silly' questions never arise.

Be yourself and don't show off. The kids will be able
to tell a mile off whether what you are saying comes

from your heart or your head, and will react accordingly.

Red herrings don't always come from the pupils either. We have had quite a few experiences where the teacher has decided to join in. Now that can be very difficult to handle, because the teacher is really in charge.

Not long ago, we found ourselves in a classroom where the teacher was doing everything he could to get the kids to react against us. He was waving his arms and shouting, 'Come along you lot! You are for ever telling me that Christianity is a load of *$!*. So why don't you tell them?' He was getting red in the face and pointing at us, and then we noticed that the kids were getting terribly embarrassed by it all. We didn't particularly mind him sounding off, but it was obvious that the class were not enjoying the display, and instead of agreeing with him they started to shout back, 'Oh shut up, sir! You're a pain and it *is* a load of *$!* when *you* tell it, but we're listening to *them!*' The whole situation swung away from him and we had to end up saying, 'Look, Mr Smith, if you have a particular axe to grind we will gladly talk to you in the staffroom afterwards, but in the meantime perhaps we could let the kids have their say.' The class (who, by the way, were sixth formers) started to applaud and came *en masse* to our concert because of this little outburst.

The sad thing was, that afterwards in the staffroom the teacher came clean and told us he was a de-frocked minister and had never been able to forgive his parishioners for the way they had booted him out.

There's a lot to the schools ministry and you have to practise much discernment. There are times when it's great for the teacher to join in the lesson and there are times when it's not.

Some teachers offer to leave the room while you take the lesson, because they feel that the kids will open up

more if they are not there. This is sometimes true, but
nine times out of ten it doesn't make much difference
once they are interested in what you are saying. We
have worked both ways and really the only reason why
it's sometimes better to keep the teacher there, is that
the pupils cannot distort the facts of what went on in
the lesson.

Chaos and calamities we have lived through

Where do I start? There are an enormous amount of
one-off situations because all schools have slightly
different ideas and practices. For us, as a band, one of
the biggest problems is to find that the only free hall to
play in is three flights up! Carrying heavy musical
equipment up three flights of stairs at quarter to eight
in the morning is no joke. Taking it down three flights
of stairs at the end of a busy day is no joke either!

Never, ever, upset the caretaker! He can be of the
greatest help to you. He knows where the light switches
are, and where the window openers are kept. He has
round pin hole adapters, plus of course *the keys to the
school*! This is imperative if you have to arrive early to
set up any equipment, because 98% of the time, no one
has told the caretaker you are coming, which means
unless you can plead your case he's not going to let you
in! And if he's just polished the hall floor, he's not
going to let you drag all that horrible equipment across
it either! So be nice to the caretaker, he has a rotten job
to do.

Most schools are terribly hospitable and will ply you
with coffee and tea and school dinners, and even this
can get you into a mess, as we have found out on
several occasions. There was one time when a teacher
offered to fetch us some coffee in the middle of a heavy
day, and naturally we took her up on the offer. Then a

few minutes later someone else came along with a
message that there was coffee waiting for us in the RE
teacher's room. Problem!

Sounds very minor, I know, but believe me, it was
days before those two teachers talked to each other
again!

There have been so many awkward times...like the
headmistress who insisted on having her chair *and*
sitting on it during our assembly at her school. I don't
know if you can imagine what it's like to actually *sit* in
front of a guitar amplifier and a set of drums while they
are going full blast.... That particular lady does—
although I doubt if she would do it again!

Then there are the teachers who insist on absolute
silence before we begin to play. Again, just try to picture
absolute silence before a rock band start up!

We've also had our fair share of headbangers, the
official anti-CU brigade, the fella who decided the Lord
had a message for the whole school halfway through
our assembly, and not to mention a couple of flashers!

So beware! You are not in the safe confines of your
local church youth group (as harrowing as that can be).
You are dealing with everyday kids!

10

More Schools Work

Our schools ministry is nationwide, and it could be
that you are looking just to serve your local area, in
which case there will be some differences in the way
you take lessons, but we hope in this second part to
give you a few ideas to work on.

We said earlier that your testimony is a good place to
start. If you are going in with someone else for a while,
then see if you can get an opportunity to give your
testimony in a classroom, guided by the other schools
worker. There is nothing like practical experience for
sorting out the things you will and will never say again!
Go over your testimony yourself and think what kind
of thing would be of interest to the kids. That doesn't
necessarily mean that your testimony has to be
flamboyant with lots of blood and gore and drug-taking.
On the contrary, they get that from every other visitor
and in every other lesson. In fact, we have been in
lessons where a pupil has put his hand up and said,
'What about the suffering in the third world?' The rest
of the class have given a great groan and thrown things
at him! Yes, I know, in your day it was, 'Please, miss,
we've done this map before!' Nowadays it's, 'Oh, miss,

do we *have* to do nuclear war again?' And that's a fact!

Kids will be much more interested in your own personal story as it happened to you. No one can deny your own story, but it does give them a chance to ask you about it, and that's where you have to decide whether you are brave enough to answer the kinds of questions kids ask.

We have been asked any number of questions like: 'Why haven't you got any children?'; 'What could God ask you to do that you wouldn't do?'; 'When you make love, do you think of God or your husband?'; 'Are your parents still together and have you made them become Christians too?'

If you take the questions seriously and answer them in an adult fashion then you will find that you have a classroom of little adults who will listen to what you are going to say next. On the other hand, if you try and get out of them, or tell them not to be so silly, you will wind up with a classroom full of little kids. Remember it is much more adult to admit you don't know the answers to all their questions, than to get yourself tied in knots with answers that don't really add up. And half the time they are only testing you to see your reaction anyway.

If you are going to be visiting the same school on a pretty regular basis then you will need to start compiling an ongoing type of lesson, so that each time you go back to the school, you can follow on from where you left off. But most of the time you will need one-off lessons. You will soon learn what the kids do and do not enjoy doing. We have found that most enjoy doing the kind of 'multiple choice' quizzes found in magazines. You know the sort of thing: 'If someone spilled drink down the front of your new suit, would you: a) Retaliate with your own drink; b) Smile and say, 'I never liked this suit anyway'; or c) Pretend it didn't happen to cover any embarrassment.'

Now the important thing about this type of quiz is that you add up your score and if you look on the next page, it tells you what sort of person you are. *That* is the bit people find fascinating. So John and I devised a multiple choice that could be used in a lesson situation with any comprehensive-age schoolkid. It works well for various reasons (which we will talk about afterwards), but first, here's the quiz:

1. When was the last time you went to church?
   a. A few months ago.
   b. Last week.
   c. Never.
   d. A wedding or funeral, etc.

2. If someone came up to you in the street and said they were God, would you...
   a. Say, 'hello!'
   b. Say, 'No you're not!'
   c. Ask him to prove it.
   d. Shake hands, just in case he is.

3. What do you think Christians should be known for?
   a. Not smoking.
   b. Being like Jesus.
   c. Never doing anything.
   d. Being nice to people?

4. Which do you believe in the most?
   a. Horoscopes.
   b. A God who holds the world together.
   c. Nothing.
   d. A force or power of some sort.

5. Do you think Jesus is...
   a. A prophet?
   b. The living God?
   c. A fairy story?
   d. A dead hero?

6. If God answered your prayers, would you want to know more about him?
   a. I might do.
   b. Yes.
   c. Not interested.
   d. If it would help me.

The scoring system

Tell the class that for every time they have answered the questions with an A, they must give themselves three points. B is four points, C is one point and D is two points.

Before you get them to add up their score, it is worth telling them that there are no winners, so the quiz should be done honestly and then they can see if they match up with the description you are going to read out.

Answers

0–8 You've probably never asked yourself whether there is a God or not, and nobody has bothered to tell you about him. This makes you the most likely contestant to become a Christian. There's a rebel in you that means you would go for it 100%.

9–15: You are content as you are, because nothing too bad has ever happened to you. Your family life is OK and although it may be a bit boring you are too lazy to find out if there's anything else to live for.

16–20: You are nice. However, being nice can also

mean that you just agree with everyone all the time in order to avoid a row. It's time you worked out your own ideas...and who to believe in is the most important one of all.

20–24: If you're not a Christian, then you probably have Christian friends or parents who have influenced your life. You sometimes feel that you would like to join them. Well, go ahead. It's the best thing you could do.

Schoolkids enjoy this kind of thing and have great fun yelling their scores across the room to each other and laughing in agreement as you read out their descriptions. Of course, the opportunity is now wide open for you to discuss some of the situations you have described...what *would* you do if someone came up to you in the street and said they were God? If there are two of you in the same classroom you could ask each other these questions and then get the kids to join in.

This multiple choice is just one idea and I'm sure you could think up many variations of it—different questions that pertain especially to your area, or different subjects with a Christian flavour.

Another idea we have worked on just lately is a quiz called 'Stop me when you know who I'm talking about'. It became clear to us that there are many famous and influential people who are Christians and who would be known to pupils, so to give them an idea of just how many famous people they know who are Christians, we devised this quiz. (By the way, if you think I'm quiz mad, well, perhaps I am, but it's a brilliant way of getting your whole audience joining in and can lead on to just about anything you want to say.)

So, the idea behind this quiz is to read out very slowly, a few words at a time, the description of someone famous, and see who in the class can recognize the personality first. Sometimes they will get it straight away, others they won't get until you reveal more clues. Obviously you try to start with obscure details that could relate to anyone. For example: He was born...in India (by now many people have shouted out Ghandi). He was christened...Harry Roger Webb (there's usually someone by now who will recognize Cliff Richard's real name and the game is over).

OK, try this one! His picture is on the wall of just about every girl's bedroom (this will cause shouts of just about everybody). He is not English (everyone turns to American pop stars). He spent three years in Bible college (outlandish guesses). He is Norwegian (a great chorus of Morten Harkett will resound across the room).

Now, if you are reading this book and you are a youth leader and you don't know who Morten Harkett is...then shame on you! But to put you out of your agony—let me tell you he is the lead singer of the group Aha. (You can add a few points to your score if, by the time you read this, they are no longer taking the charts by storm!)

As you can imagine this is more of an 'ice-breaker' than a theme for the whole lesson, but it does get the kids to realize that there are more Christians around than they first realized. You can make yourself quite a decent list of these people, including footballers, pop stars, TV personalities and sportsmen.

We have found that it is much more beneficial to talk about Jesus today and how he can affect lives, than it is to talk about Bible stories and historical bits and pieces. For a start, the chances of anyone knowing who Jonah or Abraham were are very slim indeed. Don't kid yourself that today's teenager has any kind of Bible knowledge (you may encounter awkward silences if you throw in remarks about Jonah or Moses), whereas they *will* know who Morten Harkett is. What's more, they'll be interested in what you have to say about him.

You can always find out where your class is at (especially if you are going there on a regular basis) by doing a multiple-choice quiz based on an elementary Christian theme. For example:

When did Jesus die?
a. Easter
b. Good Friday
c. Christmas
d. Pentecost

Which of these is not a book in the Bible?
a. John
b. Andrew
c. Peter
d. Mark

It may seem silly to you, but I'm sure the results will shock you.

Another thing that can be done on a regular basis, is to find a Christian book that would interest the class. We were in a school recently where my own book *I'm a Christian but...* was being used in assembly. They were taking a different theme every day. This could easily be continued in lesson time, discussing things like: 'I'm a Christian, but I find the Bible hard to read.' Or, 'I'm a Christian, but does that mean I can't look good any more?' It would help a great deal if you could find a way to make the Bible come alive to those kids. You must know yourself, if you have ever tried to read the Bible without understanding what it's about, or what Jesus was about, that it was a dry old book, especially if you tried to read it from the beginning.

Discuss the relevance of being a Christian today,

with today's fashions, today's music and today's problems. Obviously you don't have to use my book; a lot of schools are equipped with *The Cross and the Switchblade* or *Run Baby Run*. I know they've been around a long time, but gang warfare will always be a popular subject for pupils. There's also the added attraction of bringing in the video one lunchtime.

I know I have only given you a few ideas, but hopefully they will be a springboard to your own special brand of schools ministry.

Don't forget, just spend some time getting to know the kids first. Find out what they like, what they listen to, what their favourite TV programmes are, and capitalize on them for Jesus! Don't ram it down their throats—they are sick to death of people doing that to them about any number of things.

Let it come naturally. It doesn't matter if your first lesson is spent on who is going to be top of the first division this season, with just five minutes of 'What makes you a Christian?' tagged on the end. You are not there to preach and make converts, you are there to teach and make friends.

I I

The Future

This is probably one of the most fascinating subjects in the world, and Christians and non-Christians alike get very excited about it. What we would like to do in this chapter is to look forward to heaven and chat about what we think it will be like. When we hold seminars on this subject, people generally have so many questions afterwards that answering them can take twice as long as the seminar itself! A bit later on we'll be discussing some of those popular questions like: 'Will my hamster be there?' and, 'Will I recognize my gran?'

Where's it all going?

We live in a world of decay. Boring as that might seem, it's the truth. Everything wears out—even those jeans you've had since they invented Levi's—they will actually become of no earthly use to you! Isn't it annoying? And let's face it, if it doesn't wear out it becomes old-fashioned, and then you throw it out anyway. Well, just like all our favourite things wear out, so do our favourite people. We all wear out and grow old and die.

On the wall of a cemetery in Belfast someone once wrote, 'Is there life before death?' In other words, what have we got to live for? The more you think about it, the more weird life seems: you come into the world as a baby with a cry, and you go out as an adult with a groan. We spend our lives in one big routine of getting up to go to work...to earn some money...to buy some food...to give us the energy...to get up...etc, etc. Surely God intended us to get a bit more out of it than that?

Without God life can be difficult. We all have decisions to make, and some of them are major ones like: 'Where shall I live?'; 'Where do I want to work?' 'Who shall I marry?' If you are not a Christian and can't consult the Maker about these things, then you are left with horoscopes, ouija boards or even sticking a pin into a bunch of adverts!

The plan

God has a plan and a purpose for every detail of your life, and if you'll let him, he will tell you what the plan is.

I wonder what you are looking forward to at the present? Your next birthday? Christmas? Your wedding day? What have you set your heart on? Maybe these events are important, but the Lord is mapping out your future for eternity and that is a long, long time. I once heard eternity explained this way: 'If an eagle swooped down on Mount Everest, and its wing touched the very tip of the mountain once every thousand years, by the time his wing had worn the mountain down to the ground—eternity would have only just begun.'

Yes, it *is* a long time, isn't it? And the Lord wants us to fix our minds on eternity, where things don't wear out (excluding examples of mountains and eagles) and things don't grow old and die.

Sometimes we wish we could see into the future to find out what's going to happen to us, but all we need to know is, God has our best interests at heart and if we follow his plan then we will get the very best out of life while we are here on earth and in heaven later.

It's an inheritance

Matthew 6:33 is a pretty popular verse. It goes: 'But seek his kingdom first, and you can have all the other things as well.' OK, so that was the Sue Ritter version, but what the verse says and what Jesus was trying to explain was that if we would only keep our eyes on eternal things, he'd see to our earthly hassles. But being the sort of people we are, we have both eyes on what's happening next week and we don't seem to be able to look much further most of the time.

What can you see when you do look further? Hard times? Bad times? It need not be that way, because the Bible says, 'Yet to all those who received him, to those who believed in his name, he gave the right to become children of God' (Jn 1:12). So once you become a child of God, you immediately become an heir. Whatever belongs to God will eventually belong to you— unbelievable as that may sound. There are lots of verses in the Bible that tell us about being sons and daughters of the living God. Have a look at Romans 8:16–17 and Galatians 4:7.

Jesus went to prepare a place for us in heaven and it is beyond description. I know that our world here has been spoiled and everything, but basically, when you look around you, it's beautiful. But heaven . . . well how on *earth* can you describe *heaven*? I wonder if we are ready to inherit a place like that?

So what's it like?

Jesus said that heaven is too difficult to describe to mere humans like us. He said, 'If I can't explain earthly things to you and get you to understand, how do you expect me to explain heavenly things to you?' (Sorry, SRV again!)

With Christianity, a lot of things come down to faith, and we have the faith to believe that heaven is as good as God said it would be. We are told to look forward to heaven. It's going to be fantastic! I think that probably most things would be outside our human understanding—just like trying to explain video to a caveman. Maybe we will be able to eat colours and smell music! I don't know. We only have five senses at the moment, and we can't imagine anything else, so how could it possibly be explained to us?

No prejudice or inequality

There are some things we do know, however, and for a start we know that there are no favourites with God. He does away with all prejudice. The poor are the same as the rich. The pretty, the plain, the tall and the short will all be the same in heaven, because despite what we might have done or been, we will all enjoy the future God has planned for us. All are saved by faith in Christ, regardless of looks or actions.

The end of suffering

There will be no cripples in heaven, because there is no sickness there. So whatever situation you are in on earth, your health will be perfect in heaven.

There will be no orphans in heaven, because we will all have the same father. We will all be children of God.

There will be no poverty in heaven as we will share in God's inheritance. The riches of heaven will be ours.

Maybe at the moment you live in a right dump. Well, in heaven a palace awaits you. Maybe you live in a palace now, but even that will seem like a dump to the one you'll be given in heaven!

Another plus is that it will be a safe place to live in! There will be no burglars, muggers or murderers there either, because everyone in heaven will be a new creation (2 Cor 5:17).

And one of the things which I always think is really brilliant is that there will be no broken hearts—no sadness. Maybe being orphaned or crippled only happens to a minority of people, but most of us have at some time or other known what it's like to be sad or broken-hearted. Jesus heals the broken-hearted and wipes away every tear.

Proud people will not exist either! Not one person in heaven will feel like they deserve to be there...and as the song goes, when we see the nail-scarred hands we'll wish we had given him more.

Revelation 7:16 adds another important factor to the list: 'Never again will they hunger; never again will they thirst.' When I first read this I wondered whether we would have the sort of bodies that don't need food, but then I remembered that we are all to join in the great marriage supper and I must admit I was quite pleased really. It seemed a shame to stop doing something so enjoyable! (And just think. Nothing will be bad for you, so you won't have to diet or anything!)

Freedom

Yes, heaven means being free from all the things that have spoilt our own world. Sin has spoilt so much on this planet that it's hard to imagine what it must have been like in the Garden of Eden before Adam sinned. I suppose that's why people write so many songs about a perfect world.

John Lennon's 'Imagine' is a classic example of this.
A beautiful song about peace in the world: no fighting,
no different religions, no colour barriers, etc., but the
title sums it all up—all you can do is imagine. Without
Jesus, all it will ever be is a glossy dream—wonderful
but totally unreal.

The physical side

The Bible doesn't say a great deal about the physical
side of heaven. It is all a bit further than our imagina-
tion can take us. We have discussed the kind of people
who will be there, but most important of all Jesus will
be there. The mind boggles at the thought of meeting
Jesus (and I don't mean that in any way irreverently).
The term 'being at a loss for words' will serve its ultimate purpose.

In this world, if someone famous makes an appearance in public, more often than not you and I are
somewhere at the back of a huge crowd, desperately
peering over everyone's shoulders trying to see, and in
my mind that's the only way I can imagine seeing
Jesus! And yet it won't be like that at all . . . we will meet
him face to face! Can you in your wildest dreams
imagine what that will be like? No, neither can I.

What do you know?

OK, quiz time again. You can try this out at your youth
meeting some time, and then spend the rest of the
evening talking about the questions that follow.

1. In heaven will you
   a. Still grow old?
   b. Stay the same age as you were when you died?
   c. Have no age (like angels)?

Answer: Luke 20:36; 1 Corinthians 15:51–54.

2. Will you go to heaven as
    a. A slave?
    b. A son?
    c. An angel?

Answer: Romans 8:14–16; Galatians 4:7; 1 John 3:2.

3. In heaven will you have
    a. Your own body?
    b. A new body?
    c. Someone else's body?

Answer: 1 Corinthians 15:35–38; Philippians 3:20–21.

Well, don't look at me. I'm not going to give you the answers! You'll have to look them up and check if you were right or not.

Problem page

We started this chapter by saying the future is one of the most fascinating subjects around, and the thing that makes it so intriguing are questions like the following, all of which have been asked at our seminars dozens and dozens of times, by young and old alike. So you don't have to be cool and think you know all the answers, because these things are common to us all, and the answer to some of them has got to be, 'Wait and see.'

'Will my hamster go to heaven too?'

I am an animal lover and I don't like this answer any more than you do. John usually makes me go out of the room while he answers this one! So let's put it this way: there's no reason why there shouldn't be animals in heaven (the lion lying with the lamb, etc.), but they won't be the ones we left behind on earth. That is because Rover, Joey and Tinkerbell do not have souls, and Jesus didn't die for them. He certainly gave us animals to enjoy and love as company, but his salvation was for human beings only. We are not the same as animals. From the moment God breathed into man, he was different. He became capable of knowing and loving God, his Creator. He was made in the image of God (Gen 1:27). Animals were not made in the likeness of God. I sincerely hope that there will be animals in heaven, because nothing would give me greater pleasure than to be able to cuddle a tiger!

'Will we recognize each other?'

Yes. On the Mount of Transfiguration Moses and Elijah were instantly recognizable as Moses and Elijah (Mt 17:1–3). And Luke 16:22–24 tells the story of the rich man who died and went to hell. When the rich man looked up he saw Abraham and a beggar called Lazarus and cried out to them to help him. Again, he obviously recognized them. So, concerning relations and friends who have gone on before—yes, you will know them again.

'Will we have physical bodies?'

Another very interesting thought. Will we become winged beings like Christian-type angels? Well, we know that our bodies will be like Christ's—it says so in Philippians 3:21. What was Jesus' body like when he appeared to his disciples in that famous room? I suppose in appearance maybe it wasn't that different— but the key is that the disciples were terrified because they thought they had seen a ghost. Why? Because Jesus just appeared! He didn't knock on the door, or wave through the window...he just appeared in the room, defying matter. In other words, he came through the wall!

So our bodies will be immortal, eternal and able to move through different dimensions. Have a quick look through that summary in Luke 24:36 onwards. And then treat yourself to a tour round Acts chapter 1 and see how our bodies will also defy gravity!

And yet this amazing body that Jesus now had, was not just a spirit because he asked Thomas to come and touch him. And in Luke 24:39 Jesus says, 'Touch me and see; a ghost does not have flesh and bones.'

'Will we need to eat?'

We won't actually *need* to eat to keep ourselves alive, but eating, as I said before, will take place in heaven. In that same part of Luke, Jesus sat and ate fish with the disciples to prove he was not just a spirit. So if we have the same bodies then we can eat too. Ah yes, and don't forget the marriage supper of the Lamb of God in Revelation 19:9. Just imagine—everyone in heaven sitting down for a ginormous meal!

I know there are hundreds more questions to be asked, but hopefully you can get together with a group and really delve into this fascinating subject, guaranteed to keep you talking and debating all night!

Hand it over

So, in conclusion, let's look at why we are here and what we are living for. God wants us to live and work for this fabulous future that he has in store for us, and yet we still live as if everything we have going for us is down here on earth! We build up our possessions more than we build up treasures in heaven. Now just a minute. I'm not saying it's wrong to have posses- sions—that would be very hypocritical coming from someone typing a book on a word processor!

Possessions in themselves are not evil, it's just the way we look on them that can get us into trouble. I am not living for my word processor, and we shouldn't hold any possessions higher than the place we give the Lord in our lives.

So, is your future in God's hands? What have you set your heart on for this week? This year? Does God figure in your plans? Get your future right with God now, and enjoy both your life on earth and your future life in heaven at the same time!

12

How Will I Know?

This was the title of a very popular song sung by
Whitney Houston, and it asked, 'How will I know if he
really loves me?' It's the sixty-four-billion-dollar question really, isn't it? So let's go through some of the most
popular questions on love and romance. But *first*, we'd
like to take you on a romantic walk through Genesis
and one of the best love stories the Bible offers....

It all starts in Genesis 29 with Jacob who had his eye
on a beautiful lady named Rachel. Now we know that
she was gorgeous because the Bible tells us, 'Rachel
was lovely in form and beautiful.' So obviously Jacob
had good taste! But as in every romance—there was the
'other woman'...in this case Rachel's sister, Leah.
Genesis tells us that Leah was not as good-looking as
Rachel. In fact Leah had delicate eyes. She was also the
older sister, and unfortunately for her, it was looked
down upon for the younger sister to marry first, so the
pressure was on Leah.

Jacob was in no doubt that he was in love with Rachel
and when he went to ask her dad for her hand in
marriage, he was not going to take no for an answer.
Laban (Rachel's dad), however, was a quick-thinking

man and knew how to pull off a deal. So in his best
Arthur Daly voice he said, 'Look, I need some help on
the land, so if you will work for me for a while, say
seven years, then I think we can come to some agree-
able arrangement about a wedding after that!' Of
course, in the meantime, he must have been hoping to
marry Leah off and therefore let Rachel have her
husband without any family embarrassment. And for
the next seven years he had an unpaid land-worker!

They say love is blind and Jacob was certainly no
exception. He shook hands on the deal and began
working for Arthur—sorry—Laban. Now, the
romantic bit about this is a quote straight from Genesis
29:20, 'So Jacob served seven years to get Rachel, but
they seemed like only a few days to him because of his
love for her.' Wow! Can you say that about the person
of your dreams? Seven years is a long, long time!

After the seven years were up, Jacob was obviously
very eager to marry Rachel, and so he went to Laban
and said, 'OK, time's up. Where's my wife?' Laban
duly set about preparing feasts and suchlike, and then
disaster struck. Somehow Laban managed to switch
sisters on Jacob without him knowing. The Bible
doesn't tell us how this was done, but I have it on good
authority that weddings were often performed at night
and maybe it was very very dark!

The next morning Jacob woke up to find himself
lying next to the ugly sister instead of Cinderella! It
must have come as a terrible shock to him, and I can
well imagine him tearing round to Laban's house in his
nightshirt, bashing at the door and calling him all the
names under the sun. And Laban probably stood there
as cool as a cucumber and said, 'Look, mate, we can't
have the youngest daughter married off first. It's just
not done. So be a good lad and look after Leah for a
while and I'll see to it that you actually *do* get Rachel in

the end. By the way, I've got a little job for you...it'll
take you about seven years, OK?'

Right. Now let's look at Leah's side of the story,
because I think that romantically she has a lot to teach
us. First of all she has obviously been made aware of
the fact that she isn't quite such a looker as her sister.
Who knows, maybe if she hadn't had a beautiful sister,
she might not have been considered so bad herself.
Secondly, when you read through this account in
Genesis, it becomes plain that Leah fancies Jacob
herself and is determined to make this 'marriage' work.
Thirdly, she makes one of life's big, big mistakes.

She becomes pregnant.

Genesis 29:32 says, 'She named him Reuben, for she
said, "It is because the Lord has seen my misery. Surely
my husband will love me now."' I wonder how many
girls across the world have uttered similar words? It's
a sad situation and one that many find themselves in.

John and I sing a song called 'One Way Love' and it's
all about how you can't love enough for two. No matter
how much you love someone, if they don't love you
back it's not going to work, is it? Actually, the song
itself is about how much God loves us and that unless
we start giving some love back in return that won't
work either! But, you see, the message is the same, and
here we find Leah taking the ultimate step of what
almost amounts to bribery!

I don't know what possesses us at times to think that
we can buy the love of another person, or that if we
really put them in an awkward or embarrassing situation they will start waving the white flag and surrender
their undying love for us. Stupid, isn't it? You may get
someone to surrender that way—but love? I think it
will drive him or her further away than ever.

So, getting back to Leah, within verses 32 to 35 she
manages to have four sons. That's one baby per verse!

Seriously though, she is trying so very desperately to reach out to her husband. In Genesis she is quoted as saying, 'Surely my husband will love me now.' That's after the first birth...and then, 'Now at last my husband will become attached to me, because I have borne him three sons.' So even after three beautiful bouncing boys she is no nearer to Jacob's love than she was before she married him!

The outcome of all this intrigue was that Jacob married Rachel just a week after his marriage to Leah. Leah bore him lots of children and, at the time, Rachel gave him none...but it didn't make a scrap of difference to Jacob *because he loved Rachel*!

What about you?

I know it's very very difficult to find yourself attracted to someone you can't have, but you must begin to realize that the Lord has someone for you. I was watching telly the other day and they had one of those sports compilations where they put music to all the funny things that have happened in the Commonwealth Games. The record they chose to go with it was by Gerry Rafferty and the words went, 'But if you get it wrong, you'll get it right next time.' And they showed athletes taking off with javelins still attached, and pole-vaulters taking a running jump and flying through the air until the pole snaps in half...you know the sort of thing. It's funny, but at the time it really struck me that that is how a lot of people are when it comes to love.

Get it right first time!

I have never been to a 'Married Couples' Weekend'. I'm sure they are really very enlightening, but to me they sound awful. I get images of lots of couples whose lives haven't worked out together being counselled by lots of other couples who have managed to put splints and bandages on their own marriage and are hobbling along nicely thank you.

There's obviously a need for that sort of thing as so many people seem to have got it wrong first time. What am I getting at? Well, it's like this: I would rather you learn from us because John and I got it right first time and we want *you* to get it right first time too!

Questions

When John and I take seminars of boy/girl relationships, the same questions come up time and time again. A lot of them will already have been covered in the Leah versus Rachel saga, but I'd like to clear up some points. So here we go....

Is there someone especially for me?

I believe so, yes. Someday your prince (or princess) will come! But as it has been said, 'You have to kiss a lot of frogs before you find your prince!' In other words, the first person you go out with is unlikely to be the one you stay with for the rest of your life.

Recently, I got into no end of trouble for saying this, when someone read more into that statement than was really there. They seemed to think that this gave them licence to run around with every available bloke—trying them all out! Now *you* know that's not what I mean, don't you?

You also get the people who will decide that the Lord has told them who this 'one person in their life' is! The trouble is most times he hasn't told the other person involved. Then you end up with the embarrassing situation of having a total stranger coming up to you and saying, 'The Lord has told me to marry you.' I wouldn't laugh too much if I were you because it happens all the time. Much more often than you would expect. But when you think about it, surely the Lord would make it perfectly obvious to both partners if this were the case? I mean, I know sometimes the Lord has to make it clear to us that he wants us to take a particular step—but that is usually when he wants to put our faith to the test to see how much we love him... *not* because he wants to push us into some horrendous relationship.

OK, so how are we going to find this perfect romance and lifetime friend? Praying about it will help, but don't use prayer like a 'lucky dip'. In other words, don't pray, 'Lord, let the first fella I talk to tonight be the one!' Just pray about your situation—whatever it is. God does actually understand, you know. He knows that you are the only attractive unattached girl in your youth group, surrounded by a load of drips you couldn't possibly care for. He knows that you are one of seven stylish blokes in a church of 100 man-eating females. He knows you fancy the bloke in the Baptist church down the road who's already going out with someone. So why don't you tell him?

But remember that this is a private conversation between you and God, and he won't expect you to go discussing it with everyone else.

Take it easy, OK? God will bring you together if you give him time and a bit of leeway. If you start dating everyone in sight, you'll get it wrong and end up being one of the unhappy people who 'got it right next time (I think).'

It is important to note, while you are on the hunt, that your perfect partner will have the same type of interests as you, laugh at the same kind of humour, feel the same way about important social issues and like just being with you. In other words, your partner will also be your best friend.

Should I bother to get engaged?

If you feel like that about it...yes. John and I were not interested in getting engaged at all—we just wanted to get married (John proposed just one week after we had been going out together, and that was fifteen years ago). However, our parents liked the thought of an engagement and as it didn't do us any harm we went out and bought a dress ring for eight pounds.

But I think there is a lot to be said for an engagement. A friend of ours was dating a girl he knew he would eventually marry, but he was in no big hurry so one day, when it was suggested that they got engaged, he just shrugged his shoulders and said, 'Yeh, why not?' As far as he was concerned he was keeping his girl-friend happy by letting her know that they had a permanent arrangement which would eventually end in marriage maybe a year or so later. No problem.

Or that's what he thought, until a couple of days later he was presented with a food mixer. He looked quite horrified and said, 'What's *that* for?' The gift-bearer explained that it was an engagement present towards their happy future home. The guy turned pale and muttered, 'But...but...'You see, once you have let the world in on the fact that you intend to marry someone, you also open the doors to all the fanatical relations and in-laws! By the end of the week, the poor bloke was being pumped for the size of the hall for the reception, the flower arrangements, who would be best man, and so on. What he hadn't realized was that arranging a wedding takes months and months (especially if you really want that particular hall).

As it happened, they turned out to be a very happily-married couple, but it's a good warning to anyone who does just want to keep the girlfriend happy!

Here's another example which I came across quite

recently. While on tour I bumped into a girl who was really sobbing her heart out. You know what it's like in a situation like that—you don't know whether to rush over and get accused of 'interfering', or walk past and get accused of 'not caring'. So, I thought I'd take the chance and rushed up to her. After quite a few soggy hankies and a quick dash for a loo roll, I discovered that this young lady was just about to get married.

'Wedding nerves?' I asked myself. I tried asking what the problem was.

'He's such a nice guy,' she replied.

Already I knew what the problem was, so I tried the direct approach.

'But do you love him?'

'He would do anything for me,' she replied.

'Yes, but do you love him?'

'He's so kind, and we get on so well...' she faltered.

'But you don't love him,' I stated down-heartedly.

'Well, I don't know...I mean how can I not love him? He would give me the world and there's not a single thing that I could say against him.'

'Have you known him long?' I asked trying to get round to the same question again.

'Oh yes, we've known each other ages... that's why we are such good friends. Everyone expects us to marry and we've been engaged for a while and I'm marrying him in two weeks.'

This remark was followed once again by floods of tears. Knowing she was a Christian, I asked her if she had prayed about the situation. She had, but was confused about hurting someone so dear to her.

After much soul-searching we came down to the fact that as much as she thought the world of him; as much as they would be tremendously happy together, she *knew* it wasn't love, because something inside her witnessed to the fact that she was capable of giving more to the right person.

Now, in this young lady's case, engagement was the best thing that ever happened, because it gave her a breathing space.

So here we have two people in two different instances, both engaged and both realizing that a marriage was imminent. The guy in the first story could handle the situation because he was certain of his love for his girl. But for the girl in the second story, it made her face the truth.

There is someone especially for you and God wants you to be with that person. God is the same about most things—there's either the centre of his will, the very best life for you, or there's second best.

I know what I'd rather have.

Can I have sex before marriage?

Now, I'm going to keep this section short. Firstly, because I have written about it in previous books and, secondly, because the answer for a Christian is, quite simply, no.

You may not find that very helpful, but once you are married and you have not had the hassle of sleeping around, you will find that your marriage is one of complete trust and harmony, instead of a life of mistrust and deceit.

A friend said to me, 'I think that sex is God's wedding present to us.' And that just about sums it up. Don't go looking for places to draw the line. You may be able to kid yourself—but you can't kid the Lord! You jolly well know how you feel when you've overstepped the mark, don't you?

Keep sex for after your marriage and you will always thank the Lord that his way is infinitely better than yours!

OK, that's all for this chapter, but why not try this

crossword—just for fun? (Solutions on page 125.)

ACROSS

2. Give him this to finish it.
6. Just one . . . that's all it took!
7. When the dating gets too much.
10. Chewed the tea around.
11. He loves --!
12. Anger.
13. Bubbles are essential in it.

DOWN

1. Type of blonde.
2. Delight.
3. The greatest of these.
4. What every girl's looking for!
5. Average.
8. For whispering into.
9. The ugly sister.

The Noah Sketch

I hope you won't see this piece as just something tagged on to the end of the book, but if you do, don't worry, because we've called it an Appendix (that's the posh word for something tagged on to the end of a book). It's just that so many people ask us for scripts and things, and I think this is one of the best scripts I've written!

It's the story of Noah and I wrote it following the RSV version, but tried to add a little insight on how Noah would have felt. It is really a drama sketch for Christians, as opposed to outreach, but as it tells a story you could actually use it on a non-Christian audience.

I know that for myself I had heard the story of Noah billions of times, but when I read the Bible version, I found there were quite a few bits that tend to get omitted from the tale, and they are quite vital.

Preparation

This sketch is done as a radio broadcast, with each player holding the script and talking into large prop versions of old BBC microphones. This makes the sketch easy to perform as you can only lose your place—not forget the words!

Actors

Eight people are needed to perform this to its full potential, and the most important thing to remember is that the whole show is done in 'Deputy Dawg' accents. (A sort of Texas cotton-pickin', Yee-ha type of accent!)

God

The person playing God should be sat on a seat near the back of the stage, but quite visible to the audience (that is, apart from the fact that he has a sheet thrown over him). This also means that he will probably need a torch to read his script! This only adds to the insanity of it all, but you wouldn't believe how long it takes some people to sort out where the voice is coming from!

He needs a good strong Texas drawl.

Everyone else

This is Noah, his wife, three sons, Fred next door and the speaker who does the in-between bits. There are no props apart from a couple of paper aeroplanes.

Reading

Unlike most scripts, all the players read out their actions as well. For example, 'And Noah said, "Gee, Lord, I'm sorry."' This gets really silly at times, and it still makes me laugh!

OK, plan of action. I shall give you the script and the only bits you don't read out are directions which will be in italics. So without further ado... let's get started.

The Noah Sketch

NOAH: One time there was this guy named Noah. He had this shed see, and his favourite pastime was knocking these here bits of wood together.

GOD: Now this particular day he heard the voice of God speaking to him, and like most Old Testament heroes, he didn't recognize it when he heard it. God said, 'Noah!'

NOAH: 'Coming Fred!' said Noah. 'I'll be next door in two minutes...just let me nail this...Aaaaagh!' Noah hit his thumb.

GOD: And God said, 'Noah!'

NOAH: And Noah said, 'Will you cut that out, Fred? I just hit my thumb! What're you shouting for anyway, Fred? *(looks around)* Fred? Fred?'

GOD: 'It's not Fred, Noah,' said God.

NOAH: 'I can see that,' said Noah. 'I take it all back. I can't see nobody! What's going on around here?'

GOD: 'It's God, Noah,' said God. 'Can you spare a few minutes? Something important's happening.'

NOAH: And Noah said, 'Gee, Lord, I'm sorry. I really thought it was Fred. Y'see he normally lends me his lawnmower on Tuesday afternoons.'

GOD: 'Cut it out, Noah,' replied God.

NOAH: 'I normally just trim the borders,' continued Noah.

GOD: 'I want you to make something for me, Noah,' said God.

NOAH: 'Right on, Lord! Whatcha want me to do?' asked Noah.

GOD: 'I think you'd best get yourself a piece of paper and a quill,' said God.

NOAH: 'Right on!'

GOD: 'Noah, do you *have* to keep on saying that? Give it a rest will ya?' said God.

NOAH: 'Right on!' said Noah.

GOD: And God said, 'OK, let's go. *(Deep breath—then all in one go.)* I want you to make an ark of gopher wood. Make rooms inside the ark, and cover it inside and out with pitch. OK? The length of the ark is 300 cubits, the breadth is fifty cubits and height thirty cubits. Make a roof and finish it to a cubit above, and set the door of the ark on its side, make it with lower, second and third decks. Got that?'
(Slight pause.)

NOAH: 'I don't wanna seem like I'm making things hard for you, Lord,' said Noah, 'but—well, my shed is two cubits by four and I think we may have a bit of a squeeze on our hands . . . .'

GOD: And God said, 'This is important, Noah.'

NOAH: 'Right o . . . Right! What's this ark for, Lord?'

GOD: 'Well,' said God, 'it's gonna rain!'

NOAH: Now rain was unknown in these Bible days, so Noah said, 'Ah . . . what's rain Lord?'

GOD: God replied, 'It's water that will pour from the heavens for days on end!'

NOAH: 'Seems to me like I should be out there inventing the umbrella, then when it rains, I can stand on my boat and put my umbrella up! By the way,' said Noah, 'talking of boats . . . what about the sea?'

GOD: And God said, 'What about the sea?'

NOAH: 'There isn't one,' said Noah. 'Well, not for thousands of miles anyway, and it crossed my mind that a boat 300 by fifty by thirty ain't gonna float in no rain puddle!'

GOD: 'Just get on with the job, Noah,' sighed God.
(In comes Fred.)

FRED: 'Noah!'

NOAH: *(With back to Fred.)* 'Yes, Lord?' said Noah.

FRED: 'Hey it's me—Fred!' said Fred. 'What's all this Lord bit for? I know I lets you borrow my lawn-mower, but there's no need for that! Let's not get crazy about this now!'

NOAH: Noah sighed and said, 'Sorry, Fred. I thought you were God there for a minute.'

FRED: 'S'OK, Noah,' said Fred—wondering what on earth Noah was talking about. 'Hey! Watcha making this time? Another scroll rack?'

NOAH: And Noah said, 'I'm building an ark, Fred. God's gonna send a flood all over the earth and if people don't repent for the way they've been creating chaos an' all... well, they's gonna drown, Fred.'

FRED: 'Repent?' asked Fred. 'But I've done nothing wrong! I may swear a little, cheat a little, maybe tell a few lies here and there... but I ain't *evil*. No Sir! So, anyway, Noah, you're building a boat, huh?'

NOAH: 'I'm building *God* a boat!' said Noah.

FRED: 'Say, Noah, those pills the doctor gave you... you still takin' 'em?'

WIFE: 'Say, Noah,' called his wife. 'Tea's ready! It's your favourite tonight—sweet and sour olive branches!'

FRED: 'Say,' said Fred in a whisper. 'Noah's building a boat!'

WIFE: 'Gee, I just gotta stop him watching *Blue Peter!*' said his wife.

NOAH: 'I heard that! And I will watch any cotton-pickin' programme I like!'

FRED: 'Noah,' said Fred. 'How old are you?'

NOAH: Noah replied, 'Six hundred.'

WIFE: 'You'd think,' said his wife, 'that he'd have grown out of that by now.'

NOAH: 'Now you listen here!' said Noah getting stroppy. 'God has told me to build a boat 300 by fifty by thirty cubits and I'm a gonna build it!'

WIFE: And Noah's wife said, 'I liked you better when you made scroll racks. When you starting on your boat, Noah?'

NOAH: 'Just as soon,' said Noah.

WIFE: 'Just as soon as what, Noah?' asked his wife.

NOAH: 'Just as soon as I finds out what a "cubit" is,' replied Noah.

SPEAKER: Meanwhile, God had told Noah to find a male and a female of every living animal and bird, and bring it on board, so that when the rains came they could save a pair of every species and start the world again.

NOAH: 'Wife! Wife!' yelled Noah.

WIFE: 'Yes, Noah, what now?'

NOAH: 'Well,' said Noah, 'I can't seem to make these snakes tally. We seem to be an adder missing. Know where it is?'

WIFE: 'Well, one of our sons is painting the roof....'

NOAH: 'Not ladder,' groaned Noah, 'Adder! Adder!'

SON: 'We all fall down!' sang the first son. 'Hey, Dad. I'm glad I've found you. I wanna complain.'

NOAH: 'Why's that then, son?' asked Noah.

SON: 'I object to sharing my bedroom with a hippo,' said the son.

NOAH: 'I'm sorry,' said Noah. 'We all have these problems. I've got two frogs, two aardvarks, two zebras and a Belisha beacon in my room.'

SON: So the son asked, 'Swop you two aardvarks for a hippo?'

NOAH: 'No deal, son,' said Noah. 'Now go and help your brother settle the swine into room 15. It looks like a pigs' sty down there!'

SPEAKER: Meanwhile, Noah and his wife and their three sons and their three sons' wives, were beginning to realize something.

SON: 'Dad...it hasn't rained yet, has it?'

3rd SON: 'It *is* gonna rain, isn't it, Dad?' asked the third son.

NOAH: And Noah replied, 'If God said it's gonna rain,

then it's gonna rain. It's just difficult, that's all.'

3rd SON: 'Why's it so difficult, Dad?' asked the third son.

NOAH: 'Because we've never *seen* rain, have we? We don't know what we're *looking* for, do we? We might not be looking in the right part of the sky, mighten we not?' *(Looks at script in disgust.)* Who wrote this script anyway.

2nd SON: Just then in walked the second son. 'Well I'm not bothering to paint that there roof any more. It don't seem to be drying...and look at me. I'm just covered in sweat!'

(Everyone else waves their hands and moves away.)

WIFE: 'Not drying?' thought Noah's wife.

NOAH: 'Dripping?' thought Noah.

3rd SON: 'Sweat?' thought the third son.

NOAH: 'Well I'll be cotton-pickin' blowed if it ain't *raining!*' yelled Noah.

ALL: '*Yippee! Yahhoo! Rain yeh!*' etc., etc.

2nd SON: 'Ha!' said the second son. 'Just wait till I sees my friends. That'll show 'em!'

ALL SONS: 'Yeh, me too.'

NOAH: *(Seriously.)* 'Sons,' said Noah, 'I'd best tell you the reasons behind this here flood. Y'see, God was so sick of the state of the world—it was in a fearful mess. This is his way of destroying the sin. Only those that repented would be saved...and none repented other than us. You have no friends left outside any more. I'm sorry.

WIFE: And his wife explained, 'We have been richly blessed because God saw fit to save us...he knew Noah to be a godly man!'

SON: 'You mean, *everyone* will die in the flood?' asked the first son.

2nd SON: 'There will only be us left?' asked the second.

3rd SON: 'No one left alive?' uttered the third.

NOAH: 'Just us,' said Noah. 'No friends, not even Fred next door. Just us. God has done a wonderful thing in saving us and we must thank him for it. Count your blessings—all of you!'

SPEAKER: Meanwhile...thirty-nine days later....

NOAH: 'All right,' said Noah, 'now we'll try it one more time. All together, one, two, three...'

ALL: 'Rain, rain go away, come again some other day!'

NOAH: 'Nope,' said Noah. 'I guess if God says it will rain for forty days....'

ALL: 'It will rain for forty days!'

SPEAKER: It finally stopped raining, and just after Noah had celebrated his 601st birthday...they ran aground.

2nd SON: 'Land! Land! We've hit land!' shouted the second son. 'Anyone here get dizzy about heights?'

NOAH: Noah asked why: 'Why?'

2nd SON: ''Cos we've gone and landed on top of a mountain, that's why,' said the second son.

3rd SON: 'Hey!' exclaimed the third son. 'How we gonna know if the ground's dry below?'

SON: 'Got it!' said the first son. 'We'll send out a parrot, then it can fly around and come back with a weather commentary!'

WIFE: 'No, send a raven. It's more biblical,' said Noah's wife.

SPEAKER: So they sent a raven. (*Throw out paper aeroplane to audience.*)

NOAH: 'How about a dove?' asked Noah.

SPEAKER: So they sent out a dove. (*Another paper aeroplane.*)
(*One of the sons throws paper aeroplanes at drama group.*)

SON: 'Dove's back,' said the first son.

NOAH: Noah said, 'Give it a week and we'll try again.'

SPEAKER: So, a week later they sent out the dove again.

(Same routine.)

2nd SON: 'The dove's back again,' said the second son.

SPEAKER: But this time it had an olive leaf in its beak!

2nd SON: 'But this time it's got an olive leaf in its beak!'

SPEAKER: Right on!

NOAH: 'OK,' said Noah. 'One more time and it should be safe to go out!'

SPEAKER: And so for the third time ... they sent out the dove.

NOAH: *(Whistles innocently.)*

SPEAKER: A week went by ... no dove.

NOAH: *(More whistles.)*

SPEAKER: Another week?

NOAH: 'This is it!' cried Noah. 'Out we go!'

SPEAKER: And Noah made an altar to God and sacrificed burnt offerings and thanked the Lord for being saved.

NOAH: And Noah said, 'Praise the Lord!'

GOD: And God said, 'Thank you, Noah.'

SPEAKER: But what's this?

WIFE: 'Noah,' said his wife, 'what's that in the sky?'

NOAH: And Noah said, 'I don't rightly know! But it sure is pretty with all those colours and everything. What is it Lord?'

GOD: And God answered, 'It's a parrot ...'

ALL: 'No! No! It's sort of archy shaped! Yeh kind of all the colours of a thing, y'know! Yeh it's sort of rainbowy ....'

GOD: And God said, 'Ah yes! It's a rainbow, Noah. A sign. A promise that I'll never flood the earth again. Tell your children what I've done, Noah. Tell them how I saved you and that the rainbow is my promise to all mankind.'

NOAH: And Noah said, 'Praise the Lord!'

GOD: And God said, 'Right on, Noah!'

Solutions to crossword

ACROSS

2. Elbow.
6. Look.
7. Heavy.
10. Ate.
11. Me.
12. Ire.
13. Bath.

DOWN

1. Ash.
2. Elate.
3. Love.
4. Boy.
5. OK.
8. Ear.
9. Leah.

The Teenage Survival Kit

by Pete Gilbert

How can I be really committed to Jesus?
Does prayer have to be boring?
What's all this fuss about praise and worship?
What can a Christian do in a war-torn,
  money-grabbing world?

If you want to be honest with God, take him seriously and set about living your life to please him, then this book has a lot to offer you.

Pete Gilbert knows that Christianity works. That an ongoing relationship with Jesus today can be a satisfying and fulfilling experience. In this book he spells out how you can find what thousands of others are discovering: a faith that makes a difference, a real alternative to the insecure, unstable and out-of-control existence that so many call twentieth-century living.

You can survive—you can enjoy *real* life to the full, if you'll accept the challenge Jesus makes today: 'Follow me.'

Pete Gilbert co-ordinates the work of British Youth for Christ in London.

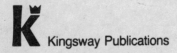

Kingsway Publications

I'm a Christian but...

by Sue Ritter

I'm a Christian but...

...surely I don't have to—
dress differently—
always go to church—
rest on Sundays—
cut myself off from the
rest of the world?

...the Bible is *so* hard
to understand—
praying isn't easy either—
witnessing isn't really for me—
I'm not baptized in the
Spirit.

Any of these complaints yours?

Sue Ritter turns her sharp eye and her
unrelenting wit to these problems—and many
others—and points the way to a successful
Christian life free from the hang-ups that can
so easily become excuses for failure.

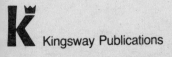

Kingsway Publications